Praise for *Chasing Planes*

"Entertaining, informative, and educational. A delightful, easy read packed with plenty of 'hangar flying,' aviation advice and life philosophy. Great gift for the 'plane crazy!'"

-Penny Rafferty Hamilton, Ph.D.,
Aviation writer and researcher

"Gordon Page brings the reader along on some of his most memorable, eclectic road trips, one colorful and character-filled aviation adventure after another. Whether he is sharing a fun, or frightening, or frustrating experience, every chapter of Chasing Planes is a captivating journey in itself. My bags are packed!"

-Ron Kaplan, National Aviation Hall of Fame

"Chasing Planes captures some great flying stories that remind me of my days ferrying planes during World War II. A must read to get a taste of the adventure of flight."

-Kathryn Gunderson,
Women Airforce Service Pilot (WASP), Class 43-W-5.

"Gordon Page is one of my favorite radio guests. His interviews are filled with great information, but it's the phone call after the show that always leaves me wanting more. Gordon's latest book, Chasing Planes, is the next best thing to that phone call."

-Matt Jolley, WarbirdRadio.com

"One of the greatest, and seemingly indispensable, talents any good pilot can master (outside of flying itself), is the ability to tell a tale. We pilots are drawn to the latest and greatest in aviation adventures and those with the ability to impart such stories with style, accuracy, and passion are even rarer than the oh-so-uncommon guy that can nail a perfect landing every single time. Gordon is the even rarer double threat… he has plenty of tales to tell and the skill to make them unforgettable."

-Jim Campbell,
CEO/ Editor-In-Chief, Aero-News Network

"If you go adventuring, you should know that there may be snakes, trucks that don't work, short trips that stretch beyond the days you planned, and those along the way who may make the path more difficult. But there will also be joy, laughter, and a sense of fulfillment that only following your dreams can bring. In that sense, Gordon Page's book, Chasing Planes, is where the love of aviation took him. More importantly, it's a book about having the courage to follow your passion. It's a great ride you don't want to miss."

-Paul Hinton, Pilot and Aviation Industry Professional

"Chasing Planes is informative and entertaining. It is a must-read for anyone whose face 'lights-up' when an airplane fly's overhead!"

-Tim Guerrero, Campus Academic Dean, Redstone College

CHASING PLANES

CHASING PLANES

Adventures of an Airplane Fanatic

GORDON R. PAGE

CHASING PLANES
ADVENTURES OF AN AIRPLANE FANATIC

iUniverse books may be ordered through booksellers or by contacting:

iUniverse
1663 Liberty Drive
Bloomington, IN 47403
www.iuniverse.com
1-800-Authors (1-800-288-4677)

ISBN: 978-1-4917-8192-0 (sc)
ISBN: 978-1-4917-8193-7 (hc)
ISBN: 978-1-4917-8191-3 (e)

Library of Congress Control Number: 2015919702

Print information available on the last page.

iUniverse rev. date: 12/02/2015

To my wife, Tracey, and my daughters, Glynnis and Callie.
Thanks for understanding why I run to the
door to see a plane flying overhead.

For once you have tasted flight you will walk the earth with your eyes turned skywards, for there you have been and there you will long to return.
–Leonardo da Vinci

Contents

Introduction xiii

Chapter One   What now Thrillbilly? 1

Chapter Two   Heli Over the Holy Land...7

Chapter Three   Vulcan to the Sky 15

Chapter Four   A Skyraider for the Collings Foundation 24

Chapter Five   Korean Sun 31

Chapter Six   A Sturmovic in Russia 42

Chapter Seven   Messerschmitt Me262 54

Chapter Eight   Fifi 63

Chapter Nine   Romanian MiG 29 74

Chapter Ten   Dayton and the Wright Brothers 82

Chapter Eleven   The Albatross and the Snake 92

Chapter Twelve   The Parts Trip 98

Chapter Thirteen   Betty's Red 112

Chapter Fourteen   The Spirit of Flight.. 121

Chapter Fifteen   Touch and Go 130

Epilogue... 153
Appendix 155
Glossary of Aviation Terms.. 175
Acknowledgements..177

Introduction

"Next up, a guitar solo from 6th grader, Randy Page," said the principal from the Delaware Elementary school in Springfield, Missouri. "Let's give another round of applause for Suzy and her baton twirling," he continued. Suzy had just mesmerized the crowd, including me, with her three minute baton routine, which was clearly going to win the school talent show. Now it was my turn to show the school what I could do. "I can do this," I told myself over and over again as I approached the stage. Suzy's baton hit my arm as she passed me on the stairs that led up to the stage.

My hands were so sweaty from nerves that the guitar slid out of my grip and hit the floor as I reached the top of the stairs. I tried to gather my composure and my memory to play *A Bridge Over Troubled Water,* a song I had practiced every day for a month prior to the talent show. I picked up my guitar and made my way to stand in front of an ancient microphone, facing five teachers who were the judges of the show. Behind them sat the entire sixth grade student body, squirming in their seats and ready to go home for the day. I was the last act and everyone, including me, was ready to leave the auditorium and head home for the weekend.

I started to strum the guitar and immediately realized that I had played the wrong cord to start the song. The judges grimaced as I recovered and moved my fingers to the right position hoping they wouldn't notice my mistake. Chord by chord I moved through the song, thinking I was doing great, but in reality I was playing the song really fast to get it over sooner. My three minute act was over in less than one minute, catching the Principal off-guard. The Principal scrambled over to the microphone from the corner of the stage as the judges shook their heads while they looked at their scoring sheets. By their actions, I had certainly not won the talent show, and my thoughts were confirmed when the Principal grabbed the microphone and said "Let's give it up for Suzy, I mean Randy." No applause came from the audience, just the sound of chairs moving on a wooden floor from anxious students ready to leave the room.

I didn't win a school talent show that day or any other, especially playing a guitar. And the only reason I even played the guitar was because my dad had crashed my control line Cox .049 powered Stuka two months before the school talent show. He gave me a guitar in the hopes I would forgive him for destroying my beloved model plane. Despite my safely flying the plane in circles hundreds of times before, Dad wanted to "show me" how to *really* fly a control line plane. On that sunny Saturday afternoon, it took just two turns, and one really steep climb, before Dad planted my Stuka into the concrete parking lot. I watched in horror as it exploded into a thousand pieces. "Guess it doesn't do a loop very well," he said as I stood in stunned silence.

My talent, starting at an early age, was anything that had to do with airplanes, not playing a guitar. Even as a sixth grader I could identify anything with wings, and as long as I could remember I have always had to look up to see what was flying overhead. On the day of the talent show as I dragged my guitar case out of the auditorium following my terrible performance, to my delight, an F-4 Phantom jet flew low over the school. I stood in awe staring at the jet as its massive engines shook the windows. "Someday that is going to be me," I told myself. I knew I could someday fly a plane, and I certainly knew that I didn't have the passion or talent to play guitar in a band.

I have spent my life chasing planes, not always an easy thing to do, and eventually made a business out of my passion for anything aviation. These are stories from my life as a pilot, consultant, broker and aircraft appraiser.

My true talent.

Chapter One

What now Thrillbilly?

"Cessna Two Kilo Delta, radar contact five miles west of the Nebraska City airport, any pilot reports are appreciated at Flight Watch, 122.0," said a controller from Kansas City Center. "Two Kilo Delta, Roger that," I responded as I piloted a 1969 Cessna 210 Centurion west after two cold days of sales calls in Nebraska City, Nebraska. I was beat and just wanted to be back at my home in Boulder, Colorado. But three plus hours of dark, winter flying were ahead of me.

The trip was one of many regular runs that my passenger Bill and I made to the Midwest to see potential clients. This had been a particularly tough trip as most of the people we met with were distracted by the upcoming Christmas holiday, and they weren't real interested in what we were trying to sell. Little did I know what real drama lay ahead of me as I climbed the 210 through 4,500' and on up to a final altitude of 8,500' for the cruise home.

Bill, our sales manager, was an adventurous, take charge type of guy, always full of energy. But on this flight he was out of his high energy management role and sat in the seat next to me as a tired passenger. It was rare for him to be tired. Nicknamed *Thrillbilly* from his days as a skydiving instructor in North Carolina, Bill wasn't afraid to do anything, and I meant anything. He had told me about his days of skydive training and bragged about the 1,500 total flying hours he accumulated over the years hauling people who jumped out of his airplanes. He had said that he hadn't flown since his days in North Carolina, but he always had advice on how I should be flying the plane when we went on our sales calls. Maybe it was because of his role as a manager that would he say, "That's not how I would do it," a common comment and one that I learned to despise. Maybe he was once a talented pilot, but I thought it was strange that he never wanted to fly the plane on our sales trips with all the flight time he had, especially since he seemed to believe he could do it better. Even though I didn't like his aviation advice, he had more flying time than me. I believed he must have had WAY more aviation knowledge than I did, so I usually went along with his direction.

As we continued west in the night sky, we saw the reflection of an early winter moon glistening off the white snow that had fallen the day before. The snow reminded me of our cold sales office in Nebraska City that had a furnace which decided to crap out during our visit. Being from dry Colorado I wasn't used to the Midwest humidity which made the temperatures seem 30 degrees colder than they actually were. I was still cold from our Nebraska visit, even though the Cessna's heater seemed to be working.

We leveled off at 8,500' near Beatrice, Nebraska, when an unfamiliar smell entered the cockpit. "Is that an electrical smell?" I asked my experienced co-pilot.

"No, just the heater." Bill responded. "Can't wait to get home," he added as he put his head against the side window and closed his eyes.

Who was I to question his wisdom? I went back to flying the plane with some cautious confidence that all was well.

A weak voice came over the Com Radio. "Two Kilo Delta, Kansas City Center, over." "Two Kilo Delta, go ahead," I responded. "Two Kilo Delta, Kansas City Center," the radio repeated. "Two Kilo Delta, go ahead," I said again, but this time I noticed that that lights on the radios had dimmed. "Two Kilo Delta, Kansas City Center. Radar is lost. If you can hear, radar service terminated, squawk VFR," said the controller. I tried to confirm the directions from the controller, but as I pushed the transmit switch all that happened was a synchronized dimming of the radio lights.

The controllers "squawk VFR" order felt more like a "good luck, you're on your own" statement.

The lights on the entire instrument panel were starting to fade as I nudged Bill in the arm to get an opinion on the situation. "Hey Bill, I think we have a problem. Think I am going to take us back to Beatrice to see what is going on." He never opened his eyes as he told me that all was okay, and to keep on pushing westward. He mumbled that in his 1,500 hours of flying he had seen lights go dim before. "Probably just a switch or something," as he put his head back on the window and motioned with his hand to keep going.

I kept flying the plane and hoped that Bill knew what he was talking about, but my gut told me otherwise as I watched the panel lights continue to fade. I glanced at the engine gauges and said a quick prayer hoping they would show no problems. Fortunately they showed that everything was working properly, but I listened closely for any little miss, knock or other hint of trouble. The last thing we needed was an engine quitting on us while we were in the dark abyss. As mile after mile passed I became full of anxiety. My mind began to play tricks on me. I felt as if someone was about to jump out from around a corner with a Halloween mask on to scare me.

The Nebraska landscape grew darker as we continued west, and the moonlight only occasionally shined off bodies of water as a reminder that land was below. I reached for my flashlight just as the panel lights flickered for the last time and the cockpit went completely dark.

"Bill!" I yelled as I grabbed the map I had in my lap.

"What's going on?" he said waking up.

"We have a problem, and it's not just a switch," I said. "We need to land."

"Are you sure?" he said.

"Yes! We are going to land."

I found the nearest airport on the map– McCook, Nebraska. Looking at the map with my flashlight, I could see that there were no tall towers between our position and the airport, so I began a descent while monitoring every sound that could mean more trouble.

"But I need to get home tonight" Bill said as the descent began.

My adrenaline was now flowing and I was pissed that Bill didn't appreciate the situation. "Well, I need to get home alive, and we're landing!" I said firmly while looking into the distance hoping to see some light.

As we descended down through 5,000', I could see some faint lights from what I hoped was McCook. The map showed the airport on the east side of town, but the only way to signal to the airport to turn the runway lights so we could see it was to click the radio on and off three times. That was a big problem for us. Our radios were dead.

I continued the descent down to 3,500, which was a good pattern altitude for McCook and planned a landing on runway 30, a nice long runway. I needed a long runway because I couldn't lower the flaps on the 210, also electric. I tossed the operating handbook for the plane toward Bill and asked him to help with the emergency checklist so we could hand pump the landing gear down. It was also electrically assisted.

That was when I found out that Thrillbilly hadn't flown a plane in over 20 years. He looked scared and said he didn't know what to do. I was on my own for sure now, so I flashed back to my flight training days and remembered the words my flight instructor said should I ever be in an emergency situation– "Stay calm, and *fly* the freakin' plane!"

Bill just sat in his seat and was somewhat catatonic. I grabbed the emergency checklist out of his hands and went though it quickly. Remaining as calm as I could, I hand pumped the landing gear until it was in a safe, down position. All I needed next was to find the airport.

I scanned the horizon east of town, hoping to see the airfield. It was too dark.

Moments later, the moon bailed me out by shining on a freshly plowed area which revealed Runway 30 at McCook Airport. With a slight right turn, I lined up the Centurion, did the final landing check and hoped that the engine would hang on a bit longer. Even though we had a higher than normal approach speed, we landed smoothly on a dark runway lined by piles of plowed snow. The snow actually helped my peripheral vision and aided me in keeping the plane going straight down the runway. As the plane slowed down, I let out a deep breath I had been holding. It was the end of my first real in-flight emergency, and we were safe.

I taxied the plane to the terminal building which was lit up inside by Christmas lights. A party was going on, and the dozens of people inside had no idea that a Cessna 210 was taxiing by in the dark. As I shut the plane down, the adrenalin rush from the flight wore off and my feet began to shake on the rudder pedals. Bill was silent. He knew that there was nothing he could say to make the situation any better.

I broke the silence by saying we needed to call a taxi inside the terminal building, find a hotel room, then a bar. So we grabbed our stuff, left the plane and headed toward the party.

I hoped I would find a sympathetic soul inside the terminal building who would hear the story of what just happened to us on our flight and understand. Instead I got yelled at to get out because it was a private party! Not what I was expecting after all that had happened that day.

I found a phone in the lobby and called The Chief Motel which was advertised on the wall. They offered a ride to the motel and sent a pickup truck with a driver who was much more sympathetic to hearing my harrowing story. Our driver said his brother-in-law ran the repair shop at the airport and he would help us out in the morning.

The next morning we hitched a ride back to the airport and were greeted by an incredibly nice mechanic who had heard about our crashing the Christmas party. It seemed we weren't the first who tried to crash the party the night before and the host had had enough.

Our mechanic inspected the 210 after we explained the situation, and he diagnosed the problem in minutes. It ended up that all of the drama the night before was due to a failed regulator which was what the electrical smell was all about. The failed regulator had caused the alternator on the plane to not work. It in turn caused the batteries of the plane to carry the electrical load for as long as they could. It was an easy 30 minute fix that got us out of McCook and back to Colorado a few hours later. Bill didn't say a word on the flight home…

I made many more sales call trips in the Cessna 210 after that Nebraska City flight, and Bill never commented or questioned me again whenever I made a flying related decision.

I think about that electrical failure situation almost every day. Most importantly, I apply what I learned that day to my everyday world. When you're on your own, try to stay calm and fly the freakin' plane of life.

Chapter Two

Heli Over the Holy Land

I have had the good fortune to have travelled the world for my day job as an aircraft broker, consultant and accredited aircraft appraiser. Through my travels, I have viewed many unique aviation collections, and have even had the opportunity to fly over foreign lands in general aviation aircraft.

A recent trip took me to Israel to inspect a WWII fighter plane. Having never been to Israel, and having grown up as a naïve American from the Midwest, my initial thoughts about going to Israel were varied. I had no idea what to expect other than a desert and holy sites. It didn't help that my mom and my wife thought I would be shot at the whole time I was there, and they didn't want me to go. My mom and my wife didn't want me to travel to Russia in the early 1990's to recover some WWII planes either. I went to Russia anyway and got back safely (kind of). So off to Israel I went.

I was surprised at what I saw as the El Al B-767 I was on approached the shores of Tel Aviv, Israel. There weren't sand dunes and camels as I had imagined, instead it looked like Miami, Florida from the air. Skyscrapers and condos lined the shoreline, and midday traffic was backed up on a modern highway system. Our plane safely arrived at a modern, beautiful airport which is named after Israel's first Prime Minister David Ben-Gurion. It rivals most of the airports I have seen around the world.

I was greeted at the airport reception area by my Israeli client and taken to a fantastic hotel just north of Tel Aviv. There weren't any sand dunes near the hotel, but there was a beach on the Mediterranean Sea where thousands of people were enjoying a summer holiday. Even though I was in Israel to work, I felt like I was on vacation thanks to a wonderful setting and the hospitality that everyone extended me.

During the third day of my trip, my client surprised me by arranging a helicopter tour of the north of Israel. The only problem was that I had been "surprised" in the past by a client in Nebraska, who because he knew I was a pilot, was sure that I would want to fly in just about anything. My client had arranged a flight in a small homebuilt plane that had scared the crap out of me. The pilot thought he would prove to me how well the plane could perform by diving under high tension power lines, brushing the tops of corn stalks and showing me how well he could stall the plane. Never again, I promised myself after that flight, but the flight in Israel was to be in a helicopter, not a homebuilt.

My client drove us north of Tel Aviv past several large kibbutz to a secluded area which was supposed to be an airport. My heart sank as we arrived to a dirt strip which was surrounded by high tension power lines. In my head it was Korea all over again. My client told me that the "airport" was for motorized paragliders and there were dozens of trailers around a run-down fabric "hangar" that stored paragliders for weekend pilots.

We waited two hours before my client received a call from the helicopter pilot who would be taking us on a tour to the Sea of Galilee and back.

The pilot had been caught in traffic and would be another hour or so before he would be at the airfield. My client felt bad about the wait and decided to take me to a local golf course to show off how green the desert can be with enough water. After a quick bucket of balls on the driving range we got a call that the helicopter was on the way, so we headed back to what I had labeled in my head as the danger zone.

An aging Russian guy, wearing only some dirty sweat pants, met us back at entrance of the field. He didn't say a word as we drove by him and a scruffy, barking dog. We drove around and found a parking spot in the dirt lot next to the fabric hangar. We waited another hour before my client said we needed to give up on the helicopter and start making some calls to see if there was a problem, or worse, a crash.

As we started the car to leave the airfield I spotted a faint silhouette of what looked like a helicopter heading toward us. As it got closer, my client turned off the car and told me that he hoped it was the right helicopter, and kept saying over and over that he had never flown with the pilot for our flight. I wasn't sure what he meant with his comment, but I was pleasantly surprised to see a fairly new Robinson 44 gently touch the dirt field and come to a smooth idle.

The pilot jumped out of the idling ship and headed toward the car. His graying hair gave me confidence that he was not a low-time paraglider pilot, but he also wasn't dressed like a corporate pilot. He wore a gray grunge band tee shirt, black shorts and a pair of black Crocs looking like he had come from the beach, not a traffic jam.

As he got closer he stuck out his hand and introduced himself as "Chibbie" apologizing for the delay and promising we were going to have a great flight. He motioned us to the helicopter saying we needed to get going as darkness was nearing.

Chibbie escorted me to the left front seat of the R-44 and my client to the back. He verified that our seatbelts were on and that the doors were locked before going to his seat to my right. We put on our headsets and Chibbie asked if I knew how to fly helicopters. "Fixed wing" I replied not knowing the pilot of the definitely not knowing the airspace. "Get out our camera and let's go," Chibbie said over the intercom. Just like the smooth landing I had witnessed we gently lifted from the dirt

We climbed out of the chopper and clearly Chibbie had been there before by the way he was greeted. We were led into a splendid restaurant where we enjoyed steak, chicken, some American country music, and wonderful views of the sea. Just as I was about to go into a food coma, Chibbie said we needed to get back into the air, especially before it got dark.

We were quickly back in the chopper and flying down the mountain like a ride at an amusement park. Chibbie flew over the sea pointing out the biblical sites where Jesus had walked on water and where the 5000 people were fed, but daylight was quickly fading as we turned toward Haifa, the third largest city in Israel. We flew down a valley that housed several large reservoirs that provide water to Tel Aviv, but not much else.

Suddenly a bright green light was shining on my left arm. It took me a few seconds to realize that it was a laser site and my blood pressure shot to the danger zone. I turned to Chibbie and while pointing to my arm asked him if this is something I should be worried about as I prayed in my head that we didn't get shot at.

Chibbie immediately started talking to ATC in Hebrew as the green laser continued to track the R-44 for what seemed like an eternity. Chibbie calmly turned to me and said that as long as we weren't being shot at that we should be okay. Well, the response wasn't what I was hoping for, but we didn't take any fire and the laser finally went off as we neared the City of Haifa.

We were in complete darkness as we flew over the Hanging Gardens of Haifa, a magnificent terraced tribute built by the Benahi Faith. Chibbie told me that this was a place that I must return to during the day to explore. "It is the eighth wonder of the world," he said. He was right, it was spectacular.

We continued our night flight along the coast of the Mediterranean Sea flying over Caesarea, a massive Roman city that King Herod had built for Caesar in 22 BC. Ruins of the Roman water ducts were visible, as were a few of the city ruins, and a newly restored amphitheater, but darkness made it difficult to truly appreciate the area.

Chibbie turned us toward the area where we began our journey earlier that day, but there was absolute total darkness and no way to see the dirt airstrip where the old Russian guy and his dog were probably sleeping by now. Chibbie turned on the small landing light on the front of the R-44 and began to circle the area saying he thought he knew where the field was, but neither of us could see a thing. I reminded Chibbie of the high tension power lines as we circled the area and he began to descend. I told Chibbie that my wife's great aunt had died in a plane that had hit a power line in WWII and I really didn't want to add to the family history that night. Besides, my blood pressure was still high from the laser incident earlier.

Chibbie's experience as a seasoned Israeli Cobra pilot was evident as he made a decision to divert to the home of the owner of the helicopter rather than risk an encounter with the power lines. He turned to the north and heading to the area he thought was correct. Soon we were flying circles with the landing light on around an area that looked as dark and as dangerous as the place we had just been. Chibbie had not landed at night at this location, but he assured me that there were not near the number of power lines as the other location, only a few...

As we were about to make another circle in the darkness, what looked like the lights of a football stadium pierced the pitch black sky. The lights were from a horse stable, and like the horses at the steak house several began to rear and run around from the sound of the helicopter. The lights went off as fast as they had come on and I noticed a small grass area where a guy stood waving a flashlight to help guide us in. Chibbie said that it was the owner of the chopper.

Chibbie masterfully put the R-44 into an area the size of my small back yard in Colorado, something I couldn't imagine doing as a fixed wing pilot. He shut the helicopter down and we jumped out in the dark onto a thick carpet of grass, a type that I had never seen before.

The owner of the helicopter greeted us and asked me how I liked the way Chibbie can fly a helicopter. "Amazing pilot," I replied, but in my head I was just glad that we had gotten on the ground safely without hitting any power lines (a dream I have had many times as a pilot) and without incident from the laser beam tracking. It was a different kind of surprise flight compared to the one I took in Nebraska, but I have to admit that I had more confidence in Chibbie than I had with my experience in Nebraska.

General aviation is alive and well in Israel. I went to the country expecting sand dunes and camels, but instead experienced the common bond of aviation despite some challenges that American pilots will hopefully never experience.

One thing is for sure, having to dodge high tension power lines and laser beams will get your heart rate up, no matter where you fly.

Chapter Three

Vulcan to the Sky

There are some incredible airshows around the world each year, and almost everyone who has been to an airshow has a memory of an aircraft or fly-by that blew them away. It is nice to see a rare plane on static display, but it is much more memorable to see a plane where it belongs, in the air, creating a life-long memory. The graceful lines of classic aircraft, as well as the sheer power and technology of modern machinery have amazed crowds that attend airshows.

Along with millions of others, I have had the life scared out of me, thanks to a rear sneak attack of an Air Force Thunderbird's F-16 that seemed to break the sound barrier while the crowds had their guard down watching a gentle formation roll. The sneaky pass usually leads to crying kids (and some adults) along with car alarms going off in the background. The pass is followed by the rapid scan of the sky to make sure another jet isn't staging to do it again. You don't forget a sneak attack!

Watching rare WWII fighters and bombers in the sky turns back time, reminding all of what happens to technology when a war requires rapid advancement. The F-117 Stealth fighter, along with jets like the F-22 Raptor, have amazed airshow patrons around the world by doing maneuvers that seem to defy the way an aircraft is supposed to move. The same goes for the mighty B-2 Spirit when it slices through the air like a giant alien boomerang, creating memories that are hard to forget.

In years of going to airshows and touring private collections and museums, I thought I had seen all of the really important aircraft that have shaped aviation history. Not so...

~~~

"This is Dr. Robert Pleming," said the man in a distinctive English accent on my voicemail. "We have an aircraft appraisal and inspection in the UK, and we hear that *you* are the guy that can do such a task. Please ring me back."

I returned the call the minute I heard the message, unaware that I was about to be introduced to one of the most incredible advancements in aviation technology that came just a few years after WWII, when the Cold War threatened nuclear destruction of the world.

"Dr. Pleming," said the man answering my call.

"Gordon Page from Denver, returning your call. How can I help?" I said.

"We need your help on an important flying aircraft here in the UK. It's the Avro Vulcan, the only flying example in the world," said Dr. Pleming.

"If we don't get a valuation, we can't fly. We *need* you, and we need you here soon," he added.

I told Dr. Pleming I could do the job and asked when he wanted me there.

"We will set up a flight the day after tomorrow and get you to Birmingham," said Dr. Pleming. "But please do your homework on the Vulcan. It is an amazing plane."

Having promised to do a deep dive on the history of the Vulcan, I hung up and got ready for a new adventure. The Cold War type.

~~~

Two days later I was standing in front of the only flying Avro Vulcan in the world. I had done my homework on the bomber, as I had promised Dr. Pleming.

The Vulcan was ominous, a jet that was built just 6 years after the introduction of the Avro Lancaster, a four-engine bomber which helped defend Britain during WWII.

The Cold War had forced the British Air Ministry to put out to bid a specification which required the design of a bomber intended to carry out delivery of Britain's nuclear-armed gravity bombs to strategic targets within Soviet territory. The new bomber needed to have a top speed of 575 miles per hour, an operating ceiling of 50,000 feet, a range of 3,452 miles and a bomb load of 10,000 pounds, all figures that were at least double what the WWII Lancaster bomber could do.

Design work began at Avro Aircraft in 1946 under Chief Designer Roy Chadwick, whose other design happened to be the famed Avro Lancaster, but this time he used a delta wing design. The first concepts featured a radical tailless delta wing design and used jet engine technology.

At the same time, design work also began at the Vickers and Handley Page aircraft factories. All three designs were eventually approved by the Air Ministry and they became the Vickers Valiant, the Handley Page Victor, and the Avro Vulcan, all known as the RAF "V" bombers.

Sadly Avro's chief designer Roy Chadwick died in a plane crash in 1947 and he never saw his second aircraft masterpiece fly. Fortunately, his work was picked up by Stuart Davies, who took Chadwick's ideas on to fruition and the Avro Vulcan, a radically huge delta wing bomber was born.

After six years of design, build and testing, the prototype full-scale Avro Vulcan VX770 first flew on August, 30 1952. It made a spectacular public appearance at the Farnborough Airshow just a few days later.

One year later at the 1953 Farnborough airshow, Vulcan VX770 led four 1/3 scale Avro 707 research aircraft and the 2nd prototype, Vulcan VX707 to the amazement of the crowd.

Despite its large size, the Avro Vulcan had a relatively small radar cross-section as it had a stealthy shape even though it had a tail fin. The Vulcan used entirely powered control surfaces which allowed use of a joystick instead of a larger yoke. The joystick system gave the pilots feedback from their control inputs.

The Vulcan normally operated with a crew of two pilots, two navigators and an air electronics operator who was responsible for all electrical equipment, a role similar to that of flight engineer on earlier propeller aircraft. Only the pilot and co-pilot were provided with ejection seats. The fact that the rest of the crew in the aircraft were not provided ejection seats, only a parachute, was a point of design criticism.

There were several instances of the pilot and co-pilot ejecting in an emergency and the rear crew being killed because there was not enough time for them to bail out of the bomber. They had to literally try and roll out the entrance door on the bottom of the fuselage.

In January, 1957 the first two Vulcan aircraft were delivered to the RAF. The training of crews started on February 21, 1957. On July 11, 1957 the RAF No. 83 Squadron received its own Vulcans and by September, 1957 several more Vulcans had been handed over to the group. A second bomber squadron was soon formed, RAF No. 101 Squadron and by the end of 1957 the last aircraft from the first batch of 25 aircraft had been delivered to them.

Ultimately 136 of this massive delta wing bomber were produced. Operationally, RAF Bomber Command and the US Strategic Air Command cooperated together in the *Single Integrated Operational Plan* (SIOP) to ensure coverage of all major Soviet targets from 1958. 108 aircraft of the RAF's V-Bombers were assigned targets under SIOP by the end of 1959. From 1962 onwards, two jets in every major RAF base were armed with nuclear weapons and on standby permanently under the principle of Quick Reaction Alert.

Vulcans on Quick Reaction Alert standby were to be airborne within four minutes of receiving an alert, as this was identified as the amount of time between warning of a USSR nuclear strike being launched and it arriving in Britain. The closest the Vulcan came to taking part in potential nuclear conflict was during the Cuban Missile Crisis in October 1962, where Bomber Command was moved to Alert Condition 3, an increased state of preparedness from normal operations, however a stand down was ordered in early November.

The only combat missions involving the Vulcan took place in 1982 during the Falklands War with Argentina. This was also the only time a V-bomber took part in conventional warfare. The Vulcans flew missions knows as the *Black Buck* raids, 3,889 mi (6,259 km) from Ascension Island to Port Stanley on the Falklands.

The first raid struck on May 1, 1982 when a lone Vulcan bomber flew over Port Stanley and dropped bombs across the main airfield. This was quickly followed up by strikes against anti-air installations made by carrier-based British Aerospace Sea Harriers jets.

After the end of the Falklands War in 1982, the Vulcan was due to be withdrawn from RAF service. However, the Falklands campaign had consumed much of the airframe fatigue life of the RAF's Victor Tankers. While Vickers VC10 and Lockheed TriStar tankers would be ordered as a result of lessons learned from the conflict, six Vulcan B.2s were converted to a tanker configuration as a stopgap measure.

The Vulcan Tanker conversion was accomplished by removing the jammers from the ECM bay in the tail of the aircraft, and replacing them with a single hose drum unit.

During the 1960s and 1970s, Vulcan bombers frequently visited the United States to participate in air shows and static displays, as well as to participate in the Strategic Air Command's Annual Bombing and Navigation Competition at locations such as Barksdale AFB, Louisiana and the former McCoy AFB, Florida. RAF crews represented Bomber Command and later Strike Command.

Vulcans also took part in the 1960, 1961, and 1962 Operation Skyshield exercises, in which the North American Aerospace Defense Command (NORAD) defenses were tested against possible Soviet air attack. Vulcans were used to simulate Soviet fighter/bomber attacks against New York, Chicago and Washington.

Sadly, many of the Vulcans that were not destroyed in accidents became the victims of the scrap yard after the decision was made to withdraw them from RAF. Fortunately, the RAF decided to use one B.Mk2 Vulcan as a display aircraft, that being Avro Vulcan XH558, which happens to be the aircraft Dr. Pleming wanted me to inspect and appraise in the UK.

Author helps put the massive XH-558 into her new hangar.

Avro Vulcan XH558 was delivered to the RAF on July 1, 1960 and at the time was painted in "anti-flash" white. The delivery flight was from the factory at Woodford, near Manchester, to RAF Waddington near Lincoln. XH558 was the first Vulcan B.Mk2 to be delivered to the RAF, and is now the oldest complete Vulcan in the world.

XH558 was also the last Vulcan to leave RAF service, flying from 1986 to 1993 as the single RAF Display Vulcan, a career of 33 years. The final flight for XH558 was on March 23, 1993 to Bruntingthorpe Aerodrome in Leicestershire after it had been sold off by the Ministry of Defense to C. Walton Ltd., a family firm who purchased and maintained the bomber with the thought that one day it might be returned to fight.

In 1997, a small team headed by Dr. Pleming started to put together an audacious plan to return her to flight, but it was clear from the start that the project would be technically challenging and enormously expensive. Not deterred, the team set off down the path that led to XH558's return to the air.

From 1998-2000, the start-up team confirmed the formal support of all the manufacturers needed to help XH558's restoration, and completed a technical review which showed there were no show-stoppers.

The real challenge was money —and first estimates were that over £3.5million would be required to pay for the restoration. Eventually a successful bid was made to the Heritage Lottery Fund, who in December 2003 announced a grant of £2.7 million for XH558's restoration, and a large grant for a sister project, the exciting new National Cold War Exhibition at RAF Cosford near Wolverhampton.

In March, 2005, XH558 was purchased for the nation of the United Kingdom by the Vulcan to the Sky Trust, a registered charity. An engineering project team, some of whom worked on Vulcans in the RAF, was assembled at Bruntingthorpe Aerodrome and they started work on the aircraft in August 2005.

Unlike certifying an EXPERIMENTAL aircraft in the United States, the Vulcan to the Sky Trust was required by the CAA to restore and operate the vintage bomber as a COMPLEX (STANDARD) category aircraft which required many more thousands of hours and adding an enormous extra expense to meet CAA standards. It was basically like rebuilding a transport airliner and having the associated expense, even though it would only fly a few demonstration hours a year. During restoration, the rudder on the fin and the elevon control surfaces on the rear of the wing all had to be re-fitted.

On the top of the wing, the metal skin had to be peeled back to expose the main structure of the wing which provides it with its great strength. This process revealed some of structure was corroded and it had to be replaced. And of course the inspection and overhaul of the four Rolls-Royce Olympus engines was a huge cost.

On August 31, 2006, XH558 rolled out of the hangar for the first time in 7 years. This had coincided with a critical funding crisis which almost shut down the restoration project, but in the last 3 weeks of August, 2006, the trust, with the drive, energy and enthusiasm of XH558's supporters in the Vulcan to the Sky Club, managed to raise over £1.3million to save the project.

In addition to the Vulcan to the Sky team, hundreds of people from all around the United Kingdom contributed to see the return of XH558 to flight.

Finally, 14 years after its last flight with the RAF and with over £7 million spent on the restoration, Vulcan XH558 roared into the air again on Thursday October 18, 2007. It was an unforgettable day for the Vulcan to the Sky team. The team said that it viewed Vulcan XH558 as a great British project, owing its success to optimism, determination, teamwork and a little bit of paranoia!

Vulcan XH558, affectionately known as The Spirit of Britain, was moved to a new home at the Robin Hood Airport in Doncaster Sheffield, UK. The bomber returned to nest in an original WWII hangar that once held up to three Vulcans at a time, a tight squeeze.

It was here that I was to do my part to save aviation history by helping with an appraisal for insurance purposes that would keep the giant bomber in the sky. Time was of the essence to get the appraisal completed so the Vulcan could be a part of the upcoming airshow season, and I couldn't let thousands of airshow fans down.

I needed to complete my inspection of the rare jet in one day to have my report to Dr. Pleming within a week.

"To help motivate you, follow me up the stairs," said Dr. Pleming as he took me up and into the cockpit of the Vulcan.

"Notice that the pilot and co-pilot have ejections seats, but not the guy looking backwards," said Dr. Pleming. "Are you motivated?" he added.

"Absolutely, but it would be better if we could fly it," I said.

"Your report will help us keep flying, otherwise, it will sit on the ground which would sadden the country." "My team will provide you whatever you need for your report," he added.

The detailed cockpit tour recounted each step that would have been taken during a Vulcan Quick Reaction Alert standby should the Soviets have launched toward the UK during the Cold War.

It was a harrowing tale that only added to the allure and mystique of the Vulcan, an aircraft that I added to my list of aviation technology that changed the world. I was motivated and finished my inspection.

Dr. Pleming made sure that I had all I needed before taking me back to the Birmingham Airport for the flight to the United States.

"Remember, we need your report to keep the Vulcan in the Sky where it belongs," said Dr. Pleming as he dropped me off at the airport. "Don't let the country down."

~~~

I finished the inspection and appraisal report in record time, thanks to the fabulous team of the Vulcan to the Sky Trust, who took me back in time to the Cold War. It was a truly once in a lifetime experience that allowed me to explore a rare, Cold War bomber inside and out.

Of the 134 Vulcans which were built, only 19 survive in the world today, and only the XH558 is airworthy thanks to the efforts of Dr. Robert Pleming, the dedicated and talented Vulcan to the Sky Trust team, and the support of donors who believe that aviation history should be seen in the air, not just on the ground.

You can help support the ambitious mission to keep XH558 flying by visiting www.vulcantothesky.org. Who knows, maybe a US/North American visit could be put together to see The Spirit of Britain in the air, to create more memories of aircraft that have changed aviation history.

You can bet that I would be there.

"Don't think about it, just get there as fast as you can," I replied.

We pulled into the FBO parking lot as the storm held its position to the west and were greeting by several FBO employees who could see the urgency on Rob's face to get the Cold War era plane into some shelter. Rob quickly ran toward a big hangar the FBO manager said would be the one to shelter the plane from the storm. Rob needed to judge the door opening with the hope that the big bird could simply taxi into the hangar with the 20 foot tall folded wings. He would taxi it because a tow bar wasn't available, and there weren't enough bodies available to push the recently fueled and incredibly heavy plane. Rob came back and asked me to climb up the beast of a plane in order taxi the short distance.

It was like a jungle gym to get into the Vietnam era plane, with several hand and foot holds to guide one to the cockpit. Rob primed the engine and turned the start switch on. It took 8 revolutions of the prop before the magnetos switched on to bring the Wright R-3350 engine to life.

A huge white cloud of smoke filled the cockpit as the engine roared to life, shaking the instrument panel to a point that the numbers on the dials were just a blur. Rob turned to me with a Cheshire Cat smile despite the urgency of the situation and said that I was really going to enjoy the next day's flight from Wiley Post to New Smyrna Beach, Florida. "You wouldn't believe how the Spad performs, even compared to a P-51 Mustang," he said. I couldn't help smiling along with Rob and knew that I was going to enjoy a trip of a lifetime.

Rob added power and taxied the plane to the open hangar as the tall rudder guided us without much need for braking. Rob folded the Skyraider's wings before easing the bird into the shelter for the night and sighed with relief as the engine shut down. "Let's hope the weather is better tomorrow," he said as we climbed out and headed back to the yellow rental car. I was certainly hopeful for good weather, as I really wanted to experience the legendary Skyraider to see if it was all he had said it was.

The next morning the weather provided us with some low level fog with broken layers of clouds, but the weather briefing said that the fog should burn off around the time of our departure. One hundred more gallons of fuel were added to a three hundred gallon center line drop tank giving us nearly six hours of endurance, but the plan was to make a stop at Meridian, MS to measure the fuel burn, and more importantly to measure the oil levels. The Skyraider holds thirty eight *gallons* of oil, and three gallons of oil were added prior to launching for our flight.

We loaded up, brought the engine to life and were quickly off Wiley Post airport, shortly before the airport went to Instrument Conditions. Rob climbed the Skyraider to 11,500' as we headed east to Meridian, MS, almost exactly half the distance to our destination of New Smyrna Beach, FL. Rob had been to Meridian before and wanted to grab fuel, along with some lunch— chili cheese dogs, waffles and soft serve ice cream.

The Skyraider performed flawlessly as it reached cruising altitude. For a big airplane it is surprising easy to fly, and as Rob promised, the handling was like a P-51 Mustang thanks to hydraulically boosted control surfaces.

The visibility in the plane is amazing for both the pilots and passengers. There is an interesting blue tint on the glass in the passenger area where Cold War electronic counter measures equipment was once installed. The cruise power settings for the Skyraider were set at 29" of manifold pressure with 2100 RPM.

as we unloaded the plane. "This plane was flown by the Commander of VAQ -33 in the Navy and is one of the rarest Skyraiders in existence. There are only four flying examples of the 218 that were built," said Rob. "Note the GD on the tail, which supposedly meant this plane was flown by God Himself," he laughed. He went on to explain that the plane now has a total of six seats, so two pilots and four passengers can fly at the same time, something the Collings Foundation wants to share with the general public.

2012 marked the 23rd year for the Collings Foundation to take aviation history around the United States, and it is with thanks to a generous benefactor who flew right seat during the trip that Collings could add the amazing Skyraider to the tour in the future (check out www.collingsfoundation.org to see the tour stops).

The Skyraider joins over 20 other planes that the Collings Foundation operates in an effort to honor veterans and enable Americans to learn more about their heritage through direct participation. The A-1E Skyraider's history, performance and sheer size is something not to be missed. It's an amazing aircraft, so don't miss it when it is on tour.

Chapter Five

Korean Sun

My hair was starting to curl on the ends thanks to the humidity in Miami. I had just arrived from a four and a half hour flight from Denver and the line to pick up my rental car was incredibly slow, leaving me sweating in the heat. The day had started not with my alarm clock, but my cat puking in the other room at 3AM. Nothing wakes you up faster than the sound of cat puke, which puts you on edge for fear that you won't step in a warm pile of puke in the dark. Fortunately it was a false alarm, just dry heaves from the cat. But I couldn't go back to sleep, so I made it to Denver International a full three hours before my flight.

Just two months before this trip, I had met a Korean by the name of Sun at a conference in Orlando. Sun and four other Koreans had stopped by our booth at a simulation conference and Sun was the only one out of the group who could speak English. Sun told me that his company was working on a new jet fighter in Seoul and they needed a product like ours to help learn to fly the new jet simulator. He went on to say that he was a former Republic of Korea Air Force (ROK Air Force) F-16 demonstration pilot.

I pulled out my computer and showed him a picture of me with a red, MiG 17 fighter jet that I friend of mine in Denver owned. He couldn't understand that someone, other than the military, could own such a machine and repeated over and over again the word, "Really?" as I described what it was like to fly the MiG. The other Koreans stood in silence as Sun and I continued to talk about the MiG until Sun excused himself from our conversation and turned to speak in Korean to his associates. "Ah," came out of their mouths in unison when they realized that Sun and I were not talking about software, but something they had all seen flying over the DMZ between North and South Korea.

Sun shook my hand as he grabbed a brochure on our product and said that he would be in touch soon. I didn't believe I would ever see him again after our brief encounter. But here I was in Miami to meet him again. Sun had set the meeting up in Miami just one day after I had returned from the Orlando conference. We could have easily met in Denver and I thought he must have had other business in Florida, which was why he wanted to meet there.

But Sun had never been to Florida prior to the Orlando trip and said he really liked the state. He wanted to see more of the Sunshine State, which is why he chose to meet in Miami. Meeting back in Florida worked just fine for me as it got me away from a nagging boss who liked to see the sales team on the road. Besides, the Rocky Mountains were in the middle of a cold winter. Sadly, it would be a fast trip to Florida and back for me. I would meet Sun for just one hour at the hotel in Miami and then turn around the next morning for a trip back to Denver for meetings at the office.

I finally got my rental car and headed to the Hilton near the Miami Airport. Upon arriving and checking into my hotel room, I noticed a flashing light on the phone. It was a message from Sun to meet him in the lobby bar at 2PM. It was 1:55PM, so I tossed my bags on the bed and headed back to the hotel elevator in my sweaty sport coat and tie.

There was no sign of Sun as I arrived at the bar, so I took a seat and stared at the menu while I waited. I waited a full hour before Sun finally entered the bar. He was wearing swimming shorts, flip flops, and a Mickey Mouse tee shirt, a far cry from the suit he was wearing when I had met him in Orlando with his team of guys. Sun greeted me with a hug and then introduced me to a lady who was dressed in a sun dress and matching high-heals. It was his wife, Lipia. She was petite, pretty and somewhat shy, but she spoke better English than Sun. After our introduction she handed a small wooden box to me and said that it was a gift from Korea. I was taken by surprise, and felt bad that I hadn't thought to bring a gift, something I wasn't used to doing, especially on what was supposed to be a business trip.

Clearly this was more of a holiday than a business trip for Sun and Lipia. I opened the box and found a patch from the ROK Air Force F-16 demo team in it. "Wow!" this is great I said. "I will have a MiG patch for you the next time we get together."

"That is why we are here," said Sun. "We want to see if it is possible to do a summer project with you."

"I thought you wanted to meet about the simulator software?" I said. "We do, but we also want the opportunity to work together on that project with the chance to fly a MiG," said Sun.

Lipia sat quietly as her visibly excited husband handed me a small gray envelope. It contained a hand-written invitation to visit Korea. "We want you to visit Korea next month," said Sun. "We want to show you our country and the company where we want to use the software," he went on. "Then you invite us to Rocky Mountains for flying."

I thought to myself, well the boss did say that he wanted us to get out on the road for sales calls, so I accepted the invitation. We sat in the bar for another hour talking about the MiG and also what it was like for Sun to fly an F-16. Lipia sat quietly as two pilots went on and on about pulling G's and afterburners.

As we exited the bar, Sun said Lipia had heard these stories many times before, which I am sure was true. She proved that fact when she rolled her eyes as we parted to opposite sides of the hotel lobby, me to my room, and them back to the pool. As the elevator door opened for me, Sun yelled across the lobby, "See you in Seoul!"

Three months later…

My boss wasn't too keen on spending the money to send me to Korea without a purchase order in hand. After all, he had paid the travel expense to send me to Miami just a few months before. Sun bugged me daily to book a trip to Seoul as apparently he also had some problems with his boss about the cost to travel to Florida-twice.

Sun had told his boss that I would be at their offices two months earlier, and they really needed to see me because the test flight of the new T-50 was to occur soon. Simulator time was a must prior to test flights, and our software would make it possible to "fly" the plane in an environment that was much safer than the sky the first time it left the ground.

It took an article in *Air and Space Magazine* announcing the new T-50 jet to get my boss to approve a trip to Korea. His desire to have our software attached to the program allowed me to book a quick, two day trip to Seoul, so off I went on a thirteen hour one-way flight to meet with Sun again.

United Airlines got me safely to the new airport in Inchon, Korea where I was greeted by Sun and Lipia once I made it to the passenger reception hall. Unlike Miami, Sun and Lipia were not dressed in pool wear, but business attire. "We need to go directly to the office to meet my boss," said Sun. "The T-50 program has stalled and we must get it back on track." I was hoping to get to my hotel to take a shower and maybe take a nap before doing anything else, but obviously it was more important to help Sun save his job than to be clean.

The drive from the airport to downtown Seoul took nearly two hours with traffic, lots of traffic. The magnificent Namsan Tower overlooked Seoul and it was hard to take my eyes off of it as we neared downtown. It seemed like every other building in Seoul had the word "Samsung" on it, and soon we were parking in front of a Samsung building where Sun worked. Sun had Lipia wait in the car as he guided me to the front doors of the building and up three flights of stairs to a room full of cubicles.

An older gentleman approached us as we entered the room and reached out his hand to me. Sun introduced him as Mr. Park, his boss. Mr. Park in broken English asked me if I had the software with me. I did have the software, but no purchase agreement to release it to him. "We need software today to keep T-50 on track," he said. Sun interjected that we were working to get it released over the next few days that I was in Seoul, after the "special tour." "Ah," said Mr. Park, in the same way Sun's team had said "Ah" in Orlando. "Well, please look around and enjoy Seoul. We will see you again soon," said Mr. Park.

Sun spoke with his boss in Korean who looked at me with a half-smile as if to say "I'll have your software soon." Sun showed me back to the stairwell and down to the car where Lipia waited. "Now back to hotel and ready for a special night," said Sun as we pulled away from the Samsung building.

We drove around Seoul on the way to the hotel, passing the Korean government "Blue House," several large crowds who were protesting against US President George Bush, the world's largest Starbucks (three stories tall), several huge shopping malls, and hundreds more Samsung buildings. We even passed the "Good Times" Motel, which certainly had nothing to do with the 1980's sitcom.

We finally arrived at the Hilton Hotel, far nicer than the sketchy looking Good Times Motel.

Sun dropped me off at the entrance and said he would be back in an hour for dinner. He added, "Then tomorrow we have a special surprise for you."

"I have heard that statement before," I said as I got out of the car hoping that the surprise wouldn't be a sight-seeing flight. I was too tired to worry about what Sun was offering and instead focused on checking in and taking a hot shower.

The hour passed quickly and I got back to the hotel lobby just in time to see Sun and Lipia pulling up to the front of the hotel in their car. As I opened the door to the rear passenger seat Lipia said "We start the night with the root." Sun just smiled as I looked at him in a way that said I had no idea what she was talking about. With little conversation, we pulled away from the Hilton and headed toward downtown Seoul.

Darkness had set in and the one thing I noticed as we drove toward the city was the number of neon crosses that lit up the tops of buildings we passed.

There were dozens of the neon crosses and I thought that maybe there were just a lot of churches in Seoul. "Hey Sun, what's with all of the crosses?" I asked.

"We all Catholic," he replied.

And that was it, no more conversation until we pulled into a concrete parking structure that was part of yet another Samsung branded building.

"We have a special guest tonight," said Sun as we exited the car and headed toward and elevator. "You get to meet The Colonel," he said as he pushed the down elevator button. "He will tell my boss to approve purchase order." Was this the surprise? I thought to myself.

Two stories down, we were inside a Sushi restaurant and we were quickly greeted by a gentleman in a suit who Sun introduced as "The Colonel." He spoke broken English, but enough to let me know that he had taken liberty to order some very special Sushi along with this favorite drink–Goldschlager. As we sat at the Sushi bar a small bowl of what looked like snot, or possibly warm cat puke, sat in front of me.

Sun said, "You will need this to make it through the night." I had no idea what he meant for me to do with the bowl of goo until Lipia picked it up and motioned for me to "drink" it.

"No freaking way!" I said to myself, thinking there was probably a bet between Sun and The Colonel whether I would or wouldn't drink it. Then two more bowls of goo were placed in front of Sun and The Colonel. They quickly picked them up and I witnessed them drink up. Lipia did not have a bowl and said she would later drive.

Now it was my turn. "You take the root," said The Colonel. "It help your stomach from what we eat and drink tonight." Despite my better judgement, and also to be respectful, I picked up the bowl, closed my eyes, opened my mouth, then I tilted the bowl. The slime went down my throat as one slick mass, but stopped half way down. It felt like it was expanding, and I was going to blow. I gasped for air through my nose praying I wouldn't blow, then suddenly down the slime ball went.

"Okay, we are ready," quipped The Colonel. After a massive Sushi dinner and a bottle of Goldschlager, maybe more, we staggered back to the car where Lipia was the designated driver. We laughed all the way home for no good reason.

Once again I was dropped off in front of the hotel. As I slid out of the car Sun said "The root will help with tomorrow when we "fry" away. Be ready at 8."

I was awakened the next morning by a call from the front desk at 8:10AM. "Your ride is here, Mr. Page." I launched myself out of bed, cleaned up in record time, then headed to the lobby. Amazingly, I felt great after the night we had! Could it have been the root?

Arriving at the lobby, Sun greeted me with a smile. He was in great shape too after the night before. "Well? How do you feel," he asked. "We have a surprise for you!"

"I'm good," I replied.

"I hope so! We are going to Top Gun today," said Sun as we walked to the front door of the hotel.

We got in Sun's car and drove over an hour to the South of Seoul where we arrived at what looked like a dirt parking lot. There were fields of corn and lots of power lines surrounding the lot, and in the middle of the dirt sat a gleaming white, super small airplane. It had a high wing like a Cessna 172, a small wooden propeller and the word, JABARU, stenciled on the vertical stabilizer. It looked like a large radio controlled plane, certainly not something a human would fly.

But then the door opened, and out jumped The Colonel! I couldn't believe he survived the night, but there he stood. "You ready to be Top Gun?" he asked.

Sun nudged me in the arm and said, "He is ready Colonel!" "Ready for what? I asked myself as Sun pushed me toward the plane.

"Uh, what's happening here?" I asked.

"We take you up, you take us up in MiG later," Sun replied.

This is where one of my life rules kicked in. Just because you are a pilot, doesn't mean you want to fly just anything or anytime. On the contrary, I pick my flying opportunities really, really cautiously and I *don't* fly home-built airplanes that I am not familiar with, especially with someone I don't know.

"Sorry, I don't fly home-built planes, but thanks anyway," I said.

"Oh, not home-built! This is a new plane from Australia from factory," said the Colonel. "I am the new dealer here in Korea. Let's go!"

The next thing I knew, Sun was buckling me into the small craft and put a CD of the theme from Top Gun into a player on the dash. "The Colonel really likes this," he said as he pressed the play button and closed the door on me.

Two people barely fit side by side in the plane and I was firmly pressed up against The Colonel as he turned the key to start the plane. It sounded like a small lawn mower engine and my anxiety level doubled as we pulled out onto a dirt road, a *short* dirt road. The Colonel added full power and we hurtled down the dirt toward a barbed wire fence that had a power line 20' above.

The theme from Top Gun blared as we barely cleared the barbed wire fence. The wheels of the plane hit the tops of the corn stalks as we gained speed, then suddenly The Colonel pulled back on the yoke pointing the plane in a steep climb. We climbed about 200 feet and I felt the plane start to stall, then The Colonel abruptly pushed the nose over and pointed us back to the ground. I was purely along for the ride, maybe my last.

Fifty feet above the corn, The Colonel pulled the plane to a level position then suddenly he banked sharply to the left, back toward the dirt lot we started from. The Colonel buzzed Sun at about 20 feet then banked sharply to the right. I was prepared to crash into the corn with The Colonel at any moment, but miraculously we climbed back to an altitude of 100 feet and were heading away from the parking lot. Then he took another sharp turn to the right and we were pointed toward the dirt road we had taken off from. The only problem, another power line and another barbed wire fence needed to be threaded to get to the dirt road, which would hopefully soon be a landing strip.

As the Top Gun theme blared, I kept saying "Please God, Please God," over and over in hopes we wouldn't hit anything wire related. The Colonel threaded the wires and cut the power to the plane. He pushed the yoke in a bit more and we hit hard on the dirt road as the Top Gun theme ended.

We turned the small plane around and taxied slowly toward Sun and his car when the night before started to kick into my head and stomach. The Colonel shut off the engine and we exited the plane as we were greeted by a smiling Sun.

"How was it?" he said.

"Well, that was some ride," I replied.

"Not bad for the first time The Colonel has flown this plane," he added. "He normally flies ROK Air Force F-16, not something like this."

I almost threw up on the spot at that statement. I broke a life rule, and it almost killed me.

The Colonel pulled out a cigarette and lit it up saying, "I am ready for the MiG now."

"Yeah, me too?" I said while the world started to spin in my head. "Let's get our software deal wrapped up and we can plan that," I added.

There was no response from the Colonel, instead Sun thanked The Colonel and excused us to go back to the car. After getting in, Sun told me that we needed to complete our "Summer Project" in order to get a purchase agreement for the simulator software. I thought about how the boss was going to react when I got back to Colorado and told him that I didn't get a purchase order, and then try to explain that I needed more money to fuel the MiG. Things were starting to not add up regarding the software deal. But for the time being, I was grateful that I had escaped a figure eight flight of death and focused on the need to get back to the hotel to clean up, then head to the airport for a long flight back to Denver, with no purchase order in hand.

Sun drove us back to the Hilton and waited for me in the lobby as I got ready for the ride to Inchon and the long flight back to Denver. As we drove to the airport Sun pushed to schedule the "Summer Project," and I reluctantly agreed to meet him in Colorado just sixty days later.

"I will bring friends with me, as well as The Colonel," said Sun. "It will be Top Gun!"

Six months later…

The wind was howling at Jeffco Airport in Broomfield, Colorado as five Koreans stood in front of a bright red MiG 17 for a photo op. The group included Sun, Lipia, and three others who worked at the Samsung simulator building in Seoul. The Koreans had flown to Denver the day before, and the group did not include The Colonel. The "Summer Project" that we coordinated in secret over the previous six months was about to begin, and my hopes were that I would soon have a sales order in hand for our software.

I had not told my boss about the adventure that was about to occur as he was pissed that I didn't bring a purchase order home from my previous trip to Seoul. He had given up on any potential sale to Korea, and oh how I wanted to prove him wrong.

Sun climbed into the MiG 17 and strapped into the rear cockpit. He would be flying with a good friend of mine, a colonel, who had heard my story of the figure eight flight in Korea and promised to return the favor to anyone I pointed out that needed a "Special Tour." The canopies closed and the colonel made a circular motion with his right index figure that the engine was about to start. The starter kicked in and the whirl of the MiG's massive engine spinning up began.

Sun sat in the back seat with a huge smile on his face as he knew that a special flight was about to happen. The sound from the jet engine got louder and louder as I looked for a sign from the colonel to pull the wheel chocks away for taxi. Then suddenly the engine power was cut and jet fuel spewed from the bottom the plane forming a huge puddle. The colonel shrugged his shoulders as the engine came to stop.

"Overtemp! Gonna need to pull the engine!" he yelled to me as Sun looked in disbelief. Sun's Top Gun flight was over, and he had never left the ground.

The colonel and Sun unstrapped from the MiG and they jumped to the ground. The other Koreans did not understand what was going on and approached Sun speaking in their language. They quickly figured out that there would be no flights in the MiG by responding to Sun saying, "Ah…"

I rescued the "Summer Project" that day by giving the Koreans, two by two, a ride in a military Beech T-42. It wasn't a MiG 17, and it certainly wasn't like the ride I had in Korea, but everyone seemed to enjoy sightseeing around Denver. The guys that couldn't speak English even gave me a thumbs up to show their appreciation.

We spent the next few days giving the Koreans rides in other types of small planes and showed them the beauty of Colorado. They returned to Korea, and Sun promised before he left that he would tell The Colonel to recommend a purchase order despite the problems with the MiG ride in Denver.

I never did get a purchase order for our software, and never did tell the boss about the Summer Project.

Chapter Six

A Sturmovic in Russia

Gary Hoffman retired from the United States Air Force as a full colonel after a 28-year career. He had held a variety of leadership positions during his time in the Air Force, and his skills in operations and management culminated with the command of all airlift and tanker support in the Pacific Theater. After retiring from the Air Force, he managed several aviation operations which included high profile and high demand clients.

I met Gary after meeting the Chief Pilot of the flight department he managed in Seattle, Washington. His Chief Pilot, Don Hitch, attended a Warbird Operators Conference I was at in Seattle just a few months before. I knew from trade journals and gossip in the warbird world, that Don and Gary's boss had a huge, and secret, warbird collection in the Seattle area.

I connected with Don over a glass of wine at the conference and I told him a story of how I literally rang the doorbell to the hangar that

I thought held the coveted warbird collection. It was the wrong hangar for the collection, but the cold call gave me a contact name, which happened to be Gary Hoffman.

Don and I hit it off at the conference having many common interest, and both of us had daughters of similar ages. Don liked the fact that I was knowledgeable about Warbirds, but really liked that I was an appraiser of the type of planes. After a few more glasses of wine, we swapped cards and I had a promise from Don to get a meeting scheduled with his boss, Gary, to see how I could get involved with the collection. It seemed that the timing to meet up with Don couldn't have been better. They needed somebody like me.

Two weeks later…

I sat by myself in a large conference room in a hangar on Boeing Field, Seattle. The meeting I had wished for was at the hangar where I had previously rang the doorbell. It did not contain a collection of Warbirds, but rather a finely tuned flight department that oversaw travel for a boss who traveled the world.

Don entered the room and introduced me to Gary Hoffman who trailed behind him. Right away, Don excused himself and left me alone with Gary, who looked like a former military officer. He was in great shape, sharply dressed, and not a single hair was out of place. "Tell me about yourself," said Gary as we sat at the massive conference table.

I provided a quick background on my business, especially my Warbird experiences around the world. After my brief overview, Gary said, "Yeah, we checked you out and you are an interesting person. Been to Russia," he added.

Our conversation was mostly small talk and lasted just half an hour. I was excused from the building and I didn't think I would be helping Gary, or anyone else related to the collection after the brief meeting. But to my surprise, I got a call the next day from Don saying that my services were needed to help with several projects, not just in Seattle but around the world. My job would be to assist Gary on the Warbird side of business, to evaluate a collection of warbirds and parts, but also to provide assistance with some restoration projects that had languished for years.

Despite years of military and corporate aviation experience, Gary needed someone like me who knew the civilian Warbird market. I was up for the challenge, and the first project was to travel with Gary to Russia and Germany to look at several languishing restoration projects.

Our trip was organized by Amanda, Gary's aide-de-camp. She smoothly booked our trip through the company travel agency, starting in Russia, ending in the UK, with a quick stop in Germany in between. At her request, I provided Amada a scan of my passport to get a travel visa for the Russia portion of the trip.

Having traveled to Russia a few times about 10 years before, I thought I knew the procedure for getting a visa. But upon receipt of my "visa," just one day before the trip, something didn't look right. My photo was attached, kind of like an application for a new passport, but the document was written in Russian and I couldn't make it out. Certainly, a ranking officer and world traveler like Gary, along with his experienced staff, knew the procedure to get a travel visa. So I reluctantly didn't question what I had received from the travel agency via FedEx.

The travel plan was for me to fly from Denver and meet up with Gary in New York at Kennedy Airport. From there, we would fly to Moscow, then on to Central Russia which contained the most interesting, but languishing restoration project which we were to inspect. A rare Ilyushin IL-2 Sturmovik. The Sturmovik was a Warbird I couldn't believe even existed, and one that I had dreamed of seeing someday. Of 36,183 examples built, only a handful were rumored to have survived, and no IL-2 aircraft were flying in world.

Early the next morning I was on a United Airlines flight to New York, my passport and visa in hand for the first segment to Russia and my first experience with Gary.

~~~

I met up with Gary as planned at Kennedy Airport at a Delta Airlines gate that had a Boeing 767 parked outside the windows. It was bound for Moscow

I felt a bit underdressed compared to Gary as I was wearing a polo shirt, jeans and some ratty tennis shoes. He was in dress slacks, button down long sleeve dress shirt, and highly polished dress shoes. I was prepared to get a military style stare down, maybe even a lecture, but Gary reached his hand out with a smile and asked how my flight was and if I was ready for Russia. I was as ready as I had been to travel to Russia. Not my favorite place, plus I had broken a promise to my wife that I would never go to the former Soviet Union again after my previous high drama experiences trying to recover WWII planes there.

But here I was, under contract, and about to see if I had a "gold star" in a file, I am sure that the Russians had on me from my prior trips.

At boarding time, Gary and I joined in the line to board the plane to Moscow. Handing our passports to an elderly male gate agent, we got a suspicious glare, and our passports and boarding passes were retained. We were asked to step aside and wait until *all* other passengers had boarded the plane. There was no obvious reason why we would have been detained, and I thought to myself, Maybe I *don't* have a gold star.

The final passenger entered the jetway, and the door to the plane was closed. I kept my cool and thought that as a former officer, Gary would be the one to take charge.

The gate agent motioned for me and Gary to approach the check-in desk. "What are you trying to pull here?" he asked.

Gary looked at me to give an answer as if he knew it was probably my fault from my previous trips to Russia. "Not sure what you mean," I replied wondering if my suspicion about the visa was justified.

"These are *applications* for Russian visa, and you can't get on the plane," said the gate agent. "No visa, no flight," he added.

"Well, so much for getting to work with you," said Gary as the agent handed back our passports and paperwork.

I didn't want to end our relationship before it had even begun, so I suggested that we try to change the trip, possibly reverse it starting in London, and maybe we could get our Russian visa processed in the UK. Gary liked the initiative to reorganize to make the trip happen, not cancel it, which would also make Gary's boss happy.

We spent the next two hours at a Delta Airlines customer service counter rearranging the trip in reverse. To make the trip happen we needed to fly from New York to Cincinnati, and were asked by customer service to retrieve our baggage from the carousel to begin our newly organized trip.

I immediately found my luggage and pulled it from the spinning platform. Gary's bag, however, was nowhere to be found. We looked until we had run out of time, then made our way to the gate for the flight to Ohio. Gary filed a missing baggage report at the check-in for Cincinnati, and was assured by Delta Airlines that it would be waiting for him in London.

We made the flight to Ohio, then on to the United Kingdom without incident. Only one problem, Gary's luggage was not in London upon our arrival. Delta tracked the bag back to a luggage carousel in New York and once again assured Gary it would meet up with him the following day. There was one more problem. Because we had changed our travel plans, there were no rooms in London to send Gary's bags to. The Wimbledon Tennis Tournament was in town and London was sold out.

Gary called Amanda to see about getting a room in London, but not even the amazing Amanda could find one.

I then remembered that my American Express card had a travel feature and took a chance by calling them to see what *they* could do. American Express came through with a room for the night, but the closest accommodations were in Brighton, a one hour train ride south of London. We had a room and a place for Gary's luggage to get delivered to, but we still needed to get to the Russian Embassy in London to get our travel visas processed. A London taxi took us across town, and we hoped that we could quickly turn our applications into approved travel to Russia.

Our hopes were crushed upon arriving at the embassy. A line of people, one hundred deep were in queue to get services, and we were told by a guard that we would have to return in three days based on the size of the line.

"Well, so much for Russia," said Gary as we turned to flag down a taxi.

But as we started to walk away from the line, a Russian gentleman approached us saying he had a "private" relationship with the embassy and his services could get us a travel visa the very next day. All we had to do was meet at his nearby office in 30 minutes, surrender our passports and visa applications, and pay him £600 each to process. Wow! The processing fee in the US was just $50 each and there was *no way* I was willing to agree to his terms.

Before I could say anything, Gary agree to do the deal. Who was I to disagree, as Gary certainly must have known what he was doing. Or did he? I thought to myself.

Thirty minutes later we were in a sketchy office where six, cigarette smoking Russian men sat shuffling papers that looked much like our visa applications. Gary and I surrendered our passports, visa applications, and a credit card for the £1200 total processing fee. I was shocked that they didn't demand cash.

We left the office with a small, hand written receipt as the only evidence of the transaction, and in my mind I was preparing myself for a future visit to the US Embassy to get a new passport. I was sure I would never see the one I had just handed over.

Gary and I made the train trip to Brighton for the night and had a pleasant stay at the hotel arranged by American Express. His luggage never made it to the hotel in Brighton, and at breakfast the next morning I noticed his formally crisp button down shirt and dress slacks were beginning to show wear from the trip. Not me, as the bag I had packed had a fresh change of clothes for each day of the trip.

I offered to share some of my clean polo shirts with Gary should his luggage not rejoin us on the trip. He appreciated the offer, but had confidence that Delta Airlines would come through with his bag. Just in case, he made a detour in Brighton to buy some underwear, then we took the train to London with thin hopes that our travel visas were ready.

We arrived back at the small, dark office near the Russian Embassy, and amazingly, the smoking Russian guy we had met the day before was there. He came through, handing us our passports with a Russian visa inside. The Russian travel visa looked like what I had remembered from my previous trip. We were good to go, so back to London Heathrow we went by taxi to head to Germany for a quick visit.

~~~

Gary's shirt was beginning to smell when we arrived in Munich, Germany. We met our contact at the passenger reception area and departed the airport by car for a quick inspection of several restoration projects that had been ongoing for three years.

On our drive to the small town near Munich that contained the projects, Gary agreed to my earlier idea of letting him wear some of my shirts, but insisted that he wear the shirts I had previous worn, not the clean ones. If no luggage showed up, Gary asked if I would agree to let him wear any extra jeans I had available. I agreed to his plan, and I instantly had even more respect for the retired colonel that had served his country with honor.

Our contact in Germany could barely understand English, but despite the language barrier, we got our inspection done in a small residential garage just outside of Munich. No wonder the project was languishing. It was a German V-2 rocket that was being restored by a single guy. The restoration work was fantastic, but it was obvious that it would be many years before the V-2 was completed.

Gary was satisfied with the inspection and said that there wasn't much else we could do, other than report back to the boss on the progress. It was the next part of our trip the worried Gary, as well as me, and after one quick night in Munich it was off to Moscow to see if our visas worked and to look at a rare piece of aviation history.

~~~

I stood in the Customs line in Moscow, just like I had nearly ten years before. Gary Hoffman was in line behind me, wearing a white polo shirt that I had on the day before. It was time to see if the visas we acquired in London would work.

A heavy set, female customs agent slowly reviewed my documents, then stamped my passport and waived me through the entrance stall without incident. The visa service in London may have been expensive, but it worked!

What hadn't worked, was Delta, as Gary was once again without luggage. I, on the other hand, thankfully picked mine up from baggage return in Moscow and promised to continue to provide Gary my daily hand me downs. He did not complain.

Boris, our contact in Russia, met us at passenger reception and quickly guided us to the exit doors in order to catch a bus to the domestic terminal building on the other side of the airport. The smoky, overcrowded bus ride was a vivid reminder that I was back in Russia, a country Gary said he had never visited, but had flown over while in the military.

We arrived at the run-down domestic terminal and checked in for an Aeroflot flight on a Tupolev Tu-134, a former Soviet military jet. Boris attempted to "upgrade" our seats and must have pissed someone off, as I ended up in a broken middle seat in the back of the plane. It was a four hour flight to Novosibirsk in Central Russia, a long four hours in a middle seat.

After arriving in Novosibirsk, we were immediately driven by a friend of Boris' to a small, two story brick building that looking like an old school. The building looked like it had barely survived World War II. It had one wall of bricks that had recently been repaired. The new bricks in the wall were in the shape of an airplane, as if it were coming toward you.

"What happened here?" I asked Boris.

"We build plane inside, then had to move it out," he replied.

"Wow," I said. "I had heard of people building a plane in a basement, then taking pieces out one by one. But a complete plane going out a brick wall?" I added. That was a new one to me.

Entering the building, Boris had Gary and I climb up a ladder to the second story of the tiny building. There were no stairs in the building. As we climbed up the ladder, Boris told us that it had been two years since the project began. The first full year was spent recovering two IL-2 center sections and six wings. Boris's company had also acquired original plans and made new, readable plans for the restoration project. The second year has been spent shaping the wooden rear fuselage and tail, and as Gary and I reached the second floor, we could look down into an adjoining room that contained what looked like a large wooden boat. It wasn't a boat, it was the Sturmovik, and the wood work was marvelous.

As we gazed down on the beautifully shaped wooden fuselage, Boris told us that the steel and aluminum center section has been disassembled for metal testing prior to rebuild. The landing gear had been inspected and they were painted and ready for reassembly. He reminded us that in Russia, all aircraft parts integrated into a flying plane must be sent out for technical inspection and certification, similar to a standard category aircraft in the US.

Boris took us into a small room where we were introduced to several engineers who were working on the project. They showed me and Gary some original steel castings for the landing gear which looked to have deep corrosion in them. But the engineers assured us that they passed inspection and were as they came out of the factory during the war, meaning rough. They said it was possible to remanufacture new castings, but there would be a loss of originality. We confirmed that original parts were key to the project.

Boris said that the next step for the project was to move it to a technical university facility to begin integration of the wooden tail section to the metal center section. That meant taking out the brick wall once again. "Is no big deal," he assured us. Boris led us back down the ladder and out the building with the promise of an authentic Russian dinner that night.

Gary responded that he really wanted to eat some local food, not some chain restaurant. Boris had just the place in mind and said that the next day we would see that university facility and the remaining pieces of the IL-2.

The authentic Russian dinner that night, was indeed authentic. Boris enjoyed an entire cow tongue that was the size of a loaf of bread. I ordered chicken to play it safe, but Gary ordered the special of the night, a fish from the Ob River which ran through the city. The fish was delivered to Gary in an odd way. It was not visible to me or Boris as it was sandwiched between two big pancakes.

Boris told Gary to pour what looked like motor oil onto the pancakes. "For added flavor," Boris said.

Gary lifted the top pancake as if he was looking under a bed for a monster. He took his fork and removed a vertebra from fish and put it on the table. Then he removed a SECOND vertebra. I told him he should have ordered the chicken, but he ate the fish despite saying it tasted funny.

Gary paid the price for eating the "special fish" that night. He didn't make it back to the hotel before having stomach problems.

The next morning we received a tour of the university facility. The guard at the entrance gate took our passports and held them while we were on the grounds. Boris took us into a dank warehouse where he showed us a large set of jigs that were in place to begin the center section assembly to the wooden tail we had looked at the day before. Several sets of mangled wings that had been recovered from crash sites were stacked up against the wall of the warehouse, but work has not begun on them.

Boris assured us that the IL-2 restoration was on track to be done soon. He showed me and Gary how his company, with the help of the university, had used a cad cam program to effectively plan the reassembly of the Sturmovik. It was impressive, but by the looks of things, the V-2 in Germany had a better chance of getting restored.

"We have another special project here," said Boris. "MiG 3," he added while motioning to follow him out of the warehouse. Inside an adjoining room sat a complete WWII MiG 3 fighter plane. "We are about to fly," said Boris. "And this start like IL-2"

Suddenly the guard from the front gate entered the room and said, "Mr. Page." My heart sank as I thought the damn visa must not have worked. "You have call, follow me," he said.

Gary looked at me in disbelief as I responded, "A call for me?" There were only two reasons in the world I could think as to why I would get a call in Novosibirsk. One was Amanda, who knew where we were and needed to get a hold of us for something. And the other possibility was the mayor of Paramushir "hearing" I was back in Russia and wanting me to return to his city in Siberia to buy some more Warbirds like we tried to years before.

As I picked up the phone, the voice on the other end was neither. It was a Warbird collector from Virginia Beach, Virginia. "Hey, it's Jerry Yagen," said the guy on a static filled phone line. "How's my MiG 3 looking?" he added.

"Uh, good," I replied not knowing how he even knew I was in Russia.

"Well, stay on top of them for me. That thing is supposed to fly soon, and it's taken years to get it done. You'll see!" said Jerry.

"Will do," I replied.

"Gotta go," said Yagen, and he hung up.

Upon returning to the room with the MiG, Boris asked me if the call was from Jerry Yagen.

"As a matter of fact, it was," I said.

"He always trying to see when his MiG is ready," said Boris. "You want to buy one?" he added.

"Not this trip. We just need to finish the IL-2 for now," said Gary.

Boris handed Gary a picture book on the MiG 3 and said, "Keep the checkbook in hand for one."

We left the university that day, and I had seen not one, but two WWII planes I had never imagined I would see in my lifetime.

~~~

Gary and I left Russia with high hopes that there would someday be a flying Ilyushin IL-2 Sturmovik over the skies of Washington State.

The Ilyushin IL-2 was an incredibly important plane for Russia during WWII. It was so important that Joseph Stalin once sent an angrily-worded cable to the IL-2 factory manager, stating, "They are as essential to the Red Army as air and bread. I demand more machines. This is my final warning!"

The inspection trip I took with Gary to Russia would be one of many I would take with him, and others in his group to support one of the most impressive Warbird collections in the World.

It was challenging work, filed with drama, but something I was more than willing to be a part of. I learned a lot from Gary Hoffman, especially when it came to how to treat other people, never to check a bag unless you really have too, and also to avoid eating weird food.

The last I heard, Gary's luggage is still on a carousel in New York.

Chapter Seven

Messerschmitt Me262

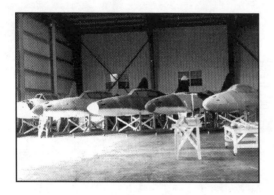

Meacham Airport in Fort Worth, Texas had been on my bucket list of aviation meccas for some time. I had heard about an old German guy on the field that could build any kind of plane, as long as he had a good set of plans. Supposedly, there were some reproduction, full size, Messerschmitt Me-262 fighter jets being built by Herb and George Tishler at the Texas Airplane Factory, and I had an hour to see if it was true, and maybe somehow try to get involved.

I pulled up to a large and unassuming, red metal hangar at Mecham Airport that sported a small sign to let visitors know that something special was going on inside the building. It was a simple red "meatball" that would have been on the side of a WWII Japanese fighter in the Pacific.

Upon entering the building, the fuselages of four Ki-43 "Oscar" fighters sat in a row, the latest projects for the Texas Airplane Factory. They were newly built planes that had been patterned from several wrecks that sat in the far back of the hangar. The wrecks were familiar to me, and the sight of them brought back vivid memories of eating raw cod liver and seaweed in the Kuril Islands of Russia. The wrecks were of planes that my Warbird Recovery group had paid for five years before, but they were never delivered to us. Instead, they were re-sold by the folks we had paid in cash, not just to the Texas Airplane Factory, but to several other buyers around the World. It was bittersweet to see those Oscars.

But my bitterness turned to excitement as I saw five German Messerschmitt Me-262 fighter jet fuselages sitting behind the newly built Oscars. They were each painted in a different scheme, and unlike the busy work on the Ki-43 aircraft, the Me-262s were staged in an almost frozen state.

George Tishler greeted me as I stood gazing at the Japanese fighters. I told him our story of the Oscar from the Kuril Islands. "Yeah, I heard about your group and what happened. Too bad," said George as his father Herb yelled something about heat treatment of part. "Set the oven to 400 degrees and try again," replied George.

"So the real reason I stopped by..."

"I know, I know," interrupted George, "The 262s. Everybody wants one," he said. "We are DONE!" he exclaimed. "They are OUTTA here!" he added.

"Well, I didn't stop by to buy one, just wanted to see if the project is real," I said.

"Yeah, it's real, but DEAD. The guy stopped paying us and we almost had to fold up shop. Thank God for the Japanese," George said.

After I asked, George let me walk around to inspect the large jets and he had no problem letting me take some photos. I had never seen any photos of the project, as the Me-262 reproductions were being built in secret, up until now.

"I gotta go back to work on the Oscars and make some money," said George as he walked away. "Have fun, and knock yourself out with them," he added.

The Me-262s reproduction jets were real, not a myth, but what was going to happen with them? I wondered if it would be possible for me to get involved.

~~~

The Messerschmitt Me 262 is a complicated jet fighter. It's big, has a stunning design, and the influence of the plane can still be seen in contemporary combat aircraft. Its swept wings, automatic slats and modular construction were all leading advances for the time. More than any other aircraft of its day, the Messerschmitt Me 262 was a fighter of absolutely unrivalled potential.

It took vision, passion and a lot of money to re-create a Messerschmitt Me 262, the first production jet, and first production fighter jet in history.

The new build Me 262 would not have been possible if it were not for the late president of Classic Fighter Industries, Stephen L. Snyder. Steve Snyder was a master aviator, an accomplished aeronautical engineer, an inventor, an industrialist of distinction and a world record-holding skydiver who dedicated his entire life to aviation.

Having developed an appreciation for Messerschmitt's jet fighter in childhood, Snyder set out to do something that others could only dream about. He wanted to accurately build flight-worthy examples of the Me 262. He began to seriously consider how such a thing might actually be done, and ultimately formed Classic Fighter Industries, Inc. with this project in mind. It then became a simple matter of waiting until the time, place, and circumstances were right to begin such a massive undertaking.

From the beginning, there was little interest by Steve Snyder in creating a plane that only *looked* like a Me 262. His objective was to create precision duplicates of the original jet fighter. However, there were significant technical challenges to overcome. Of the 1400 Me 262 that were built, only a survived, and they were scattered around the world. On top of that, technical drawings were incomplete.

Without a master pattern to follow, a reproduction Me 262 simply could not be done. What was desperately needed for Steve Snyder to achieve his dream, was an original Me 262 that could be torn apart, analyzed, and duplicated, piece by piece. Nothing less would work.

An ideal candidate aircraft was found in an unlikely setting. A solitary example of an un-restored and original Me 262 was sitting outside of Willow Grove Naval Air Station in eastern Pennsylvania. The aircraft, once known as "White 35," was a rare *Luftwaffe* trainer, complete with dual-controls.

Having spent decades on outdoor display, the jet was deteriorating rapidly. Unless it could be properly restored, its days were clearly numbered. This made it the single best hope for use in a restoration/reproduction project. It was soon discovered that the U.S. Navy owned the aircraft, but they lacked the resources to give the old Messerschmitt a quality restoration.

Recognizing the possibilities, Snyder entered into a two year negotiation process with the U.S. Navy. The Navy was offered an attractive proposal by Snyder. The proposal would permit the Messerschmitt to be dismantled and used as a template, and in return the Navy would get back a fully restored aircraft at no cost to the government. The Navy accepted Snyder's deal, and the search for a suitable fabricator began.

Originally, plans called for subcontracting all new aircraft construction to a private group in Germany, however a requirement to keep the "reference aircraft" owned by the U.S. Navy within the United States forced Snyder to find an alternate contractor. After a review of several potential restoration groups, Snyder contracted the Texas Airplane Factory in Fort Worth.

Herbert Tischler owner of the Texas Airplane Factory had the expertise needed to build the jets. Tischler quickly agreed to take on the project. He submitted formal cost estimates and began setting up a production timetable. With Texas Airplane Factory on line as the prime initial subcontractor, construction began on July 1, 1993.

The Me 262 Project, as it was code named, was at last a reality.

~~~

As work began on the Me 262 Project at the Texas Airplane Factory, a deep examination was completed on the Navy owned pattern aircraft. Texas Aircraft Factory assembled the jigs and fixtures necessary to build to aircraft and technical drawings were arranged. Many of the drawings had to be reverse-engineered.

Fabrication on the fuselage, wings and cockpit tubs began almost immediately. Each component presented a new challenge.

Fuselage components were the first to be fabricated and for the most part, they were easily copied from the original aircraft. The fuselage sections had a large number of parts that involved a lot of custom fitting as they were assembled.

Many of the wing fixtures and jigs were completed early in the project, but the actual assembly of the wings was a complex process.

One of the most important aspects of the Me 262 Project was the extraordinary engineering and design work that went into integrating authenticity with safety. In a desire to create a worthy duplication of the original aircraft, a number of ultra-low profile improvements were developed which greatly enhanced operator and flight safety.

The biggest change was the use of a modern engine. A Learjet type CJ-610 or military J-85 version replaced the original and unreliable Jumo 004. This change was just one of many to modernize the original jet fighter.

By mid-1996, the classic lines of the Me 262 jets were clearly in evidence, and the fuselage structures were nearly complete. The jets progressed to a fairly advanced state, although much work remained, especially on the wings, engines, and aircraft systems. Work slowed on the jets around the time the first two were sold—one to a judge in Arizona and the other to the Messerschmitt Foundation in Germany. Time was of the essence to keep the construction of the jets going, but more importantly, keep the cash flow flowing.

Trouble hit the Me 262 Project in mid1998 when Steve Snyder stopped paying Texas Aircraft Factory and made the decision to move the 262s to Paine Field in Everett, Washington.

I had walked into Texas Aircraft Factory the day they were notified about the move. It was not good timing on my part.

~~~

Steve Snyder had contracted with a former Boeing Senior Vice President, Bob Hammer, and in 1999 the five reproduction Me 262s were transferred to Paine Field in Everett, Washington for the final phase of the project. Even before the assets were on hand, a team of some 20+ hand-picked, paid and volunteer staff were made ready by Bob Hammer.

There is a very high level of aviation expertise in the Seattle area, and the project quickly made extensive use of a network of subcontractors. Steve Snyder recognized the production distribution method immediately and often joked that the team in Seattle appeared to be in the process of building "Boeing 262s." This was in part a reference to the high population of former Boeing specialists involved in the effort, but more to the point, it was also a nod of approval to Bob Hammer's masterful approach to project management.

The dream of reproduction Me 262s belonged to but one man in the beginning, Stephen L. Snyder, an aviation pioneer in every sense of the word. No one had worked harder, devoted more time or committed more of their personal fortune to recreating the Me 262. Sadly, tragedy struck in late June 1999 when Snyder was killed in an F-86 *Sabre* crash near his home in New Jersey.

After seven years of dogged determination and close oversight, the most central figure of the entire program was dead at the age of 64. Speculation ran wild that the project was over, even though it was making great progress with Bob Hammer's team. The Snyder family was quick to quell the mounting tide of rumors when it was announced that the project would continue in accordance with Steve's wishes. In order to stabilize the effort and set the stage for long term success, two courses of action were identified.

First, it was decided that only those jets with contracts against them would remain in an active production status. The remaining airframes would re-enter an active status only after a purchase order had been issued.

Secondly, the groundwork was laid to transfer ownership to CFII's preexisting customers. These parties formed the WTMF organization to facilitate a formal change of responsibility, and a transfer agreement was signed in early 2001.

The Me 262 Project moved forward, even as new technical challenges continue to appear on a near-daily basis. The restoration of the original reference aircraft was completed in the fall of 2000, and that aircraft was returned to its home at the Willow Grove Naval Air Station in Pennsylvania. The fact that this aircraft had arrived from Fort Worth stripped and without any documentation of the teardown process, forced Hammer's team to take frequent breaks to consult with leading experts and historians who were virtually all affiliated in one way or another.

The restoration of the original pattern Me 262 was completed in grand fashion, and the Navy took delivery of their prize according to the terms of the 1993 agreement.

In January 2003, Bob Hammer's began flight testing of the first Me 262 reproduction (Werk Number 501241) that belonged to the judge in Arizona. The success of the test flights of Werk Number 501241 would allow for the delivery of more Me 262s, including at least two B-1c two-seater variants, one A-1c single-seater and two convertibles that could be switched between the A-1c and B-1c configurations. All of the reproduction Me 262s are powered by General Electric CJ-610 or military version J85 engines, and the new build Me 262s feature additional safety features, such as upgraded brakes and strengthened landing gear. The "C" suffix in the type of configurations refers to the new type of General Electric power plants. This change was informally assigned with the approval of the Messerschmitt Foundation in Germany. The Werk Numbers (serial numbers) of the reproductions also pick up where the last wartime produced Me 262 left off, a continuous airframe serial number run with a 50-year production break. Flight testing of the judge's Me 262 did not come without some challenges, including a gear collapse on one the flights. After concluding a faulty design in the main landing gear, Bob Hammer's team made repairs to the plane and flight testing was successfully completed to the judge's delight. But there was cautious optimism from other potential buyers due to the accident, and sales of the other available planes did not come in.

~~~

Bob Hammer and his team were great engineers, but they weren't great sales people. At the conclusion of the flight testing of the first plane, I contacted Bob Hammer in Everett to offer my services as a broker to the Me 262 Project. I knew how to sell, and I wanted to be a part of a program that was making aviation history once again.

An agreement was quickly drawn up, and I began contacting everyone I could think of around the world who might be qualified and interested in owning a Messerschmitt Me262. It was not an easy task to convince would-be buyers that the issues with the landing gear on the Me 262 had been resolved.

The successful flight testing of the second Me 262 (Werk Number 501244) was evidence that the landing gear issues had been taken care of by Bob Hammer's team. The jet was disassembled and delivered by a newly built Boeing 747 to the Messerschmitt Foundation in Manching, Germany. This aircraft conducted a private test flight in late April 2006 in Manching, and made its public debut in May at the German ILA Airshow in 2006. It was the first time in over 60 years that a Messerschmitt Me 262 had flown in the skies over Germany.

Sales of the remaining Me 262s were difficult and slow, but another flying example was eventually sold to a collector on the East Coast.

Me 262 Werk Number 501241 was eventually donated to the Collings Foundation as White 1 of JG 7, and this aircraft began offered ride-along flights starting in 2008. I had spent two years promoting the idea of a ride program with Collings and had hoped that they would purchase one of the remaining planes.

However, the judge was in poor health and he, along with his family made the decision to donate the plane to the Foundation. The judge passed away, just weeks after the donation was completed. The third replica, a non-flyable Me 262 A-1c, was sold to the Evergreen Aviation & Space Museum in May 2010. It is proudly on display near the Spruce Goose. I was proud to have been a part of that sale and the sales of the other Me 262s, all from a one hour visit to Meacham, Texas, years before.

The last Me 262 reproduction, sits in storage, awaiting its turn to be completed to flying condition.

Chapter Eight

Fifi

The noise from the radial engines of four Aero Shell sponsored T-6 Texans kept the heads of thousands turned to the skies over Oshkosh, Wisconsin. The afternoon airshow was underway at the 2013 EAA AirVenture, an event that drew over 500,000 visitors from around the world during the week long show.

I stood on a taxi way near show center watching the T-6s do a four ship aileron roll in perfect harmony, when suddenly guy who was trying to walk and watch the show at the same time ran into me. "Sorry, Man," said the guy, who was wearing a tan flight suit, baseball hat, and thick Ray Ban sunglasses.

"No problem," I replied and turned my attention back to the whine of a Pratt & Whitney R-985 as a T-6 did a low pass.

"Gordon?" said the guy who ran into me.

I turned back around and looked closer at the guy as he pulled off his Ray Bans.

I glanced down at the name tag on the flight suit and read—STEVE SWIFT, B-29.

"Steve?" I replied, as we gave each other a hand shake, followed by a man hug.

"Been a while," said Steve as he replaced his sunglasses. "What are you doing here?" he added.

"Guest speaker for Bendix-King, and just looking at some planes," I replied. "And what, need I ask, are you doing here?"

Steve pointed at his name tag, then to a four-engine, B-29 Bomber sitting at center stage, awaiting its turn to fly in the show. "Flying Fifi!" Steve said.

"You have come a long way from our days of flying a B-25," I said adding a pat on his shoulder.

"You have no idea," said Steve. "Meet me after the show right here and let's catch up. Gotta run! See you in a bit," he said as he lifted up a caution-tape barrier fence and walked toward the only flying B-29 in the world, a plane I had only dreamed of flying in.

I waived at Steve and went back to gazing at the noisy T-6s that were starting to break off from formation to enter into a landing pattern.

It had been a great week for me as a guest speaker at an event that annually drew hundreds of thousands of like-minded aviation folks, like me, to tiny Oshkosh. And the odds of literally running into someone I had previously flown B-25s with was slim.

I watched Steve and the rest of the B-29 crew climb into Fifi, the lone name painted on the side of the bomber, and fifteen minutes later the engines were turning. I had never seen a B-29 in the air, and that void in my life was about to change.

The B-29 taxied out from show center and down to the end of Runway 28, while thousands of fans waived at the plane in anticipation of its take off.

Once lined up on the runway, full power was added to the Super Fortress, and the earth shook as its four Wright R-3350 engines delivered power to massive 16' diameter propellers which pulled the plane into the air.

Fifteen minutes, and three fly-bys later, the B-29 returned to earth thanks to a picture perfect landing by my friend, Steve.

Fifi taxied back to the spot it was parked earlier, and the engines were shut down as the airshow crowd cheered in appreciation. The show was over for that day, and as promised, Steve returned to meet up with me.

"Well obviously you are having more fun than me at the show," I said to Steve as he walked up to me.

"Maybe," he said with a big smile on his face. "That was a horrible landing," he added.

"Looked great to me, but who am I to judge," I replied.

"Hey, I don't have a bunch of time, but were coming to Denver next Friday for the airshow. Can you get to Sioux Falls and help us out?" Steve said while rolling up the sleeves on his flight suit.

"What do you mean?" I said.

"Just get your butt out to Sioux Falls by Thursday night, and we'll get you up front the next morning," replied Steve.

Without any hesitation, I agreed to be in Sioux Falls, hopeful that Steve was serious that I could get up front, or anywhere for that matter, in the only flying B-29 in the world. "Hell, I'll do the windows!" I said.

"Just be at Joe Foss Airport and ready to go no later than 8AM next Friday, or you'll be airlining it back to Colorado," he said. "Gotta go," Steve added, as the rest of the B-29 crew joined him for a walk to waiting golf cart that said B-29 CREW on the side.

My week had just gotten even better, and thoughts were racing in my head about booking a flight to Sioux Falls for the flight of my life.

~~~

It was easy to book a flight to Iowa once I was back in Denver, but not so easy to convince my wife that I had to be back on the road after being gone the previous ten days. She knew that my "work" in Oshkosh was more like a vacation, especially with all of the planes and other aviation related venues I had been "subjected" to.

"Just go," she said when I begged her to let me fly to Sioux Falls for the flight of a lifetime. It didn't matter to her that I had the chance to be in a mega-rare plane. "Guess I'll get everything ready for the airshow at Jeffco this weekend on my own while you go play with your friends," she said.

I promised her that I would be back in time to prepare a mobile museum display we had committed to our friends Jim and Scott, the directors of the largest airshow in Colorado. They had worked hard for a solid year to get the rare B-29, and a B-24 Liberator to the show as the headliners, and our mobile museum would add to the show. I was sure one or both of *them* would be in Sioux Falls for the ride to Denver and told my wife my thoughts. "Just go have fun," she said. I played her approval down on the outside, but inside I was jumping for joy at the thought that I was going to take a flight of my life.

~~~

The flight to Sioux Falls was nothing like the previous one and only other flight I had taken to the small Iowa town. This time I was on a United 737 in the economy section. The last time I had flown to Sioux Falls had been in a P-51C Mustang with my friend Rob Collings. We had flown from Fort Collins, Colorado to Sioux Falls to meet up with the Collings Foundation tour that included their B-17 and a B-24. That was one of the "just go have fun" trips that I had billed to my wife as a "working trip." Actually, it is a lot of work to be on the road with the Collings Foundation Tour. It is more like being a gypsy, moving from town to town with the planes, and working your butt off to keep the old birds in the air.

This flight, I was in a middle seat, drinking a bad cup of coffee and rather than complain, I tried to focus on the joy of a flight in the B-29 the next day.

The United 737 touched down in Sioux Falls on time, despite a heavy rain storm that was in the area. Rain would be a factor for the B-29 flight if it didn't clear out the next day, as the plane was only rated to fly in clear conditions.

A taxi took me to a Holiday Inn in downtown Sioux Falls where I checked in, along with a large crowd of high school kids that were in town for a softball tournament. It was a long, sleepless night at the Sioux

Falls Holiday Inn with a lot of screaming and laughing going on in the halls. But like on the flight, I tried to stay focused on happy thoughts the B-29, but I have to admit, I had some thoughts of what I could do to get back at the hotel for giving me a room on the same floor as the team.

~~~

It was raining as I arrived by taxi the next morning at Maverick Air Center. The B-29 sat out on the ramp, along with a B-24, water dripping off the control surfaces, which made the odds of my dream flight diminish. I saw Steve and the rest of the flight team in their flight suits huddled in the middle of the passenger waiting area as I walked into the FBO.

"Hope you have a return airline ticket," said Steve as I approached the group.

"Yeah!" in unison said a two familiar voices from the vending machine area. It was my brother Paul, along with one of our Spirit of Flight museum Board members, Paul Gordon.

"What are you guys doing here?" I said.

"Hopefully flying back to Denver in the B-24," said my brother.

Paul Gordon added, "Yeah, the airshow director, Jim, was supposed to be on board today, along with a TV lady. She bailed, and he decided that he should stick around to set up the airshow in case the weather was bad."

My brother said, "Good timing for me! I was at the airport yesterday when that all went down, and was offered an open seat. Here I am! Was gonna rub your nose in it, but noooo," he added.

The same had happened with Paul Gordon, who had a huge camera around his neck. "I'm going to take a *ton* of pictures," he said.

"What are you flying on?" he added.

"B-29, supposedly," I replied.

Steve joined us at the vending machine and said "We *might* be able to get out of here in four or five hours. Weather is going to break up. Stick around," he said while walking back to the B-29 team.

I had a choice of sticking around for the flight in the B-29, or catching a flight that departed in four hours back to Denver. If I missed the United Airlines flight, I could be sitting in Iowa for days until the weather cooperated. My wife would be pissed if I didn't get back to help out for the airshow. But the B-29 flight was something I just couldn't pass on, so I gambled that we would be flying that day and decided to wait it out in the terminal.

~~~

Four hours later, a United 737 took off in a rainy mist as I watched from the picture windows of the FBO. The rain had slowed from earlier, and Steve approached me with an IPad in hand. "We are going to have a tight window, but I think we can make a move in about an hour. Get your stuff ready," he said.

The rest of the group that had been lounging on the chairs in the lobby the last four hours slowly started make their way to the planes. This included my brother and Paul Gordon.

"There's been a change," said Steve. "Gordon's brother and the photographer are now on the B-29." "Get checked in," he added.

My brother and Paul Gordon were elated and made their way with me to a check in table in the adjoining hangar which had a one P-51 Mustang sitting in the corner. "Oh if only I could fly that," I thought to myself as my brother jumped in line ahead of me, thinking he would be a better seat by checking in first.

At check in, we signed a liability form, and everyone was assigned a "position" on the plane. Each was given a lanyard with a laminated position name on them. "I got the waist gunner" said my brother as he waived his lanyard in my face. "Where are *you* sitting?" added. It was like we were kids again and he was teasing me.

There was only one lanyard left when it was my turn to check in for the flight. "Wow, you must know somebody," said the lady at the check in table. You are in the cat seat!

I looked at the lanyard which said BOMBARDIER on it. "You are in the best seat in the house for this trip," added the check in lady. "Get your camera ready."

I didn't wave my lanyard at my brother, but could see on his face that he was ready for me to do so after he heard what the check in lady said.

"Gordon!" yelled Steve. "You remember what you said about doing windows? Get out there and help!"

"Yessir!" I replied as I walked out of the hangar into a windy, but no longer raining staging area for the bombers.

I met the co-pilot for the day and was immediately asked to hold a ladder while he jumped up and cleaned windows on the pilot's side of the B-29. He cleaned all of the windows while I made sure the ladder didn't blow over in the wind. The rest of the group that was flying that day stood around waiting for the words to load up. The B-29 and B-24 flight crews hurried about, inspecting the aircraft and pulling propellers through to get any accumulated oil out of the bottoms of the radial engines.

"We're gonna go!" yelled Steve as the clouds started to break up.

There was a mad rush by the flight crews to get passengers on board of the bombers in order to take off for Denver. My brother and Paul Gordon were guided by a crew member to the rear of the B-29 with the rest of the passengers as Steve told me to stick by him.

"Told ya, you would be up front," Steve said. "Let's go," he added, motioning to a ladder near the front landing gear of the plane.

It was time to fly.

~~~

Steve and the co-pilot, along with a flight engineer who faced backward, took their places in the cockpit. The flight engineer was busy with a wall of engine gauges as Steve and his co-pilot leaned back in their seats, pulled down the brims of their baseball hats, crossed their arms and looked like they were about to take a nap. "Nothing we can do just yet," said Steve. "Check out the Norden," he added, pointing to a device sitting in the glassed-in nose for the plane.

The bombardier seat that Steve had arranged for my dream flight was a bit intimidating. There was a wall of glass, similar to the picture windows in the FBO. A small seat belt was all that would hold me into position while a top secret Norden Bomb site was mounted in front of my position. To the left of me was a metal box with stenciled lettering that read: Bombardier's Check list. I couldn't resist and pulled the check list out of the box. There were but three items on the checklist. 1. Look Down. 2. Aim At Japan. 3. Remember Pearl Harbor.

It was a great way to begin the journey from Iowa to Colorado.

Steve and the co-pilot perked up as the flight engineer said that he was ready to start the first engine. "Here we go," said Steve.

I could see from my seat that the propeller of engine number three began to turn. A huge plume of blue smoke from residual oil blew out of the engine nacelle as the engine came to life. Things were now happening in the cockpit as the flight engineer shouted out numbers to Steve.

Engine number two was started and we started the taxi to the end of the runway with just the two engines running. I hadn't noticed that the B-24 was already rolling for take-off at the end of the runway, and it lifted off as we tuned onto the taxi way. "They're slower," yelled Steve. "Gotta give them a head start."

Rain clouds were starting to form up again as we neared the end of the taxi way. The flight engineer started the other two engines as Steve yelled out, "We gotta go before the rain."

We lined up on the runway and power was added in unison to the four Wright 3350 radial engines. The plane shook from the power of the engines as the plane slowly moved forward. The B-29 used up all of the runway on the take-off roll before it lumbered into the sky, just a few hundred feet over a golf course adjoining the Sioux Falls Airport.

The B-29 made an ever so slight right turn toward the downtown area of Sioux Falls and within minutes we were directly overhead of the Holiday Inn I had stayed in the night before. I couldn't help myself and looked into the eyesight of the Norden Bombsite just as we passed overhead. The Holiday Inn was my Pearl Harbor that day.

Steve kept the B-29 under the deck of the clouds as we turned to the west toward the Rocky Mountains. "Shouldn't be too long before we find a hole to climb through," Steve yelled. "The '24 found a spot," he added as he moved the yoke of the B-29 back and forth.

"You can head on back," Steve said. "Go check her out."

I was hoping to visit every inch of the B-29 on the flight, so I unbuckled myself and headed to the back of the plane, first stopping by the navigator's position. Protected by a sheet of plastic was the hand written signature of Theodore "Dutch" Van Kirk, who was the Navigator on the Enola Gay B-29. It was a surreal feeling as I looked at the signature, and it truly impacted me as I made my way to the back of the bomber.

I made my way through the pressure vessel, through the bomb bay, and into the rear of the B-29. Its engines hummed like I had only heard in movies, but this was real.

I found my brother at the waist gunner position as Paul Gordon stood on a platform gazing out of the top turret of the bomber.

My brother motioned with excitement for me to join him where he sat. "Hurry, hurry," he yelled. "P-51!" he added, while snapping photos with his phone.

I pulled myself around the top turret platform and joined my brother as a North American P-51 flew in formation with the B-29. It was the one that was in the corner of the hangar in Sioux Falls! It had caught up to the B-29 without any problems. "A passenger in the back said it's coming to Denver!" said my brother as he continued to take pictures.

I left my brother and hurriedly headed to the back of the Superfortress to see the rest of the bomber. I wanted to get back to the cat seat to take my own pictures of the Mustang.

As I approached the rear of the plane, a gentleman said that I would have to crawl on my hands and knees to get to the rear gunners position. "Don't miss it!" he said as I lowered myself to begin the journey to the farthest rear position of the plane.

As I crawled to the back of the plane, I could hear the whistle of wind coming through an opening of the fuselage. Suddenly, my lanyard got sucked though an opening below my position. The lanyard pulled my neck down toward the opening, which is where a tiny tail skid would normally have been retraced into place. Adrenaline took over and without hesitation I reached down and pulled the lanyard out of the air. Enough of that, I thought to myself and I crawled backward back to where I had started.

The guy I had passed on the way to the tail gunner's position said, "That was fast! Great, right?" he added.

I didn't answer and made my way back to the front of the plane, passing my brother who continued to gaze at the Mustang from the gunner position.

I walked through the bomb bay and back to the front of the plane, only to find a guy sitting in the Bombardier's seat that I had planned to return to in order to photograph the P-51. Steve stopped me before I could pull the guy out of my seat and said that he was an organizer of the airshow in Sioux Falls. "Let him sit there for a while," Steve said. "The organizer of the Denver show was supposed to be in that seat today," he added.

I stood gazing at the Mustang though a small, scratched up window, unable to take a clear photo, and hoping the guy would vacate my seat in time to get a picture or two.

He sat in my seat until 20 minutes outside of Denver, and I never did get a clear picture of the now long departed P-51.

Seeing my frustration, Steve told the organizer guy that he needed to take his assigned seat, and I got to sit back down in the bombardier position just in time for the B-29 to form up with the B-24 for the final approach and landing at Jefferson County Airport.

As we flew over the airport for an initial approach to landing, I could see that a large crowd had gathered to see that bombers and to welcome them to the airshow.

Steve greased in the B-29 and once again complained about his landing. He taxied the massive bomber to an area on the ramp that had been opened up for the bombers to park. As we approached the ramp, a guy waiving orange batons guiding us to a final shut down area. It was the airshow director, Jim, the guy who was supposed to be on the B-29 flight that day.

As we taxied closer, Jim noticed that I was sitting in the bombardier's position, the spot he had been scheduled to sit in that day. Unlike me, he couldn't risk not being at the airshow and did not take the chance on weather.

I was lucky that the weather had worked out to get a flight on the B-29 that day, something that I had dreamed about as a kid. I later heard that it was a dream of Jim's too.

As the engines shut down on Fifi, Jim smiled, and I could see him slowly mouthing the words—ASSHOLE.

Chapter Nine

Romanian MiG 29

I was awakened from a deep sleep by the sounds of the Adhan that was being called out by a muezzin via a loudspeaker from a mosque that was down the street from the hotel I was staying at in Bucharest, Romania. Having grown up in Colorado I had never heard singing or a call to prayer like this. And up until now, the closest in my life for a call to prayer had been my mom telling me to get my butt out of bed and get ready to go to church.

Sleeping in was on my mind after the long flight to Romania the day before, but I needed to get my butt out of bed to get ready for a long drive to the Black Sea to look at a project for a client of mine. So, with beautiful singing in the background, I dragged myself out of the hotel bed and got ready for what promised to be an interesting next few days. I was on the hunt for a Russian MiG 29.

It had taken months to put this trip together, and it had to be arranged through a contractor who had been doing business in

Romania the past two years. It would have been impossible for me to have coordinated the players on my own, so I had contacted an old friend who had been involved in some high end military contracts, and he knew the right people to help me find a MiG 29 for a client.

Tom was my friend, and he perfectly fit the mold as an F-15 fighter pilot. He was clean cut, tough, firm and a proud Eagle driver. I hadn't seen Tom since he had given me a private cockpit tour of his F-15 at the Reno Air Races two years before. It was in Reno that I learned what Tom's call sign was- HEAVES. I had asked him how he picked that call sign, and was told that you don't *pick* your call sign in the military, it's given to you by others, and the call sign generally comes from an event and when you least suspect.

It was a tradition, as was the tradition of being called out at a bar to show your challenge coin, or buy a round of drinks if you didn't have your squadron coin in your pocket. A night of heavy drinking had resulted in Tom's call sign…

Tom stood in the lobby of the Bucharest hotel as I made it down from my room. I needed coffee to get my morning kicked into gear, but Tom looked like he had already worked out, had breakfast and was ready for a mission.

"I am burned out," I told Tom as I grabbed a cup of coffee in the front lobby.

"Well get ready to go "FLASH," we gotta a MiG to look at," said Chris.

He had just given me a call sign.

Just then, another guy joined me at the coffee urn.

"This is Charlie," said Tom. "My contact who put this together."

"Good to meet you," Charlie said, as he grabbed a Styrofoam cup of coffee.

"We have some driving to do, so let's go." Tom seemed to be all business.

Tom and I followed Charlie to his car that was waiting at the front doors of the hotel. We drove 163 miles with little talk as we passed small towns, rolling countryside and an occasional Gypsy family pulling an RV behind a horse.

We arrived at the entrance gates of an Air Base in Constanta, Romania near the Black Sea. Two cars were stopped at a security booth that we would have to pass to enter the base. A diplomatic car along with a military intelligence car were being thoroughly searched at the guard shack.

Once it was our turn, we presented our passports to the guard, who then made a call to the base commander. We were asked to park our car near the guard shack and to get out of the vehicle. We waited only a few minutes before the base commander drove up in his personal car to meet us.

We were waved in past the diplomatic and MI groups and our car was not even searched. It seemed that Tom had certainly arranged the trip with someone who had incredible connections.

Tom knew his way around the facility and there seemed to be some excitement around the base with lots of cleaning of the building exteriors, lawn mowers trimming grass, and the grooming of gravel roads. We were soon parking in front of the main administration building.

Charlie escorted me and Tom into the administration building and into a large waiting area where we were greeted by a waiting by the base commander, who quickly lit up a cigarette. "Would you like one?" he asked. We all passed on the offer.

"NATO summit is coming," said the commander, which explained the efforts to visually enhance the base grounds.

"I am very busy," said the commander. "But my chief assistant will escort you to anything you wish to see," he added, while taking a drag from his cigarette.

As he exhaled to create a smoke plume, a gentleman dressed in military fatigues walked into the building.

"This is my chief assistant," said the commander. "Despite security from NATO summit, he will show you everything."

"I must go now," said the commander waiving us to the exit of the building.

The chief assistant escorted us out of the building and asked Charlie in broken English to follow him to a hangar on the other side of the base.

We drove closely to the chief as we passed barracks, administration and maintenance buildings. All of the buildings had personnel that were busy outside working on appearances.

We pulled up to a large hangar, and unlike the other base buildings receiving attention, the hangar was run down and in need of repairs.

Upon entering the building, the chief said that the facility was no longer supporting jets. "It is now used to fix helicopter," said the chief, who then introduced us to a gentlemen he identified as the senior MiG 29 maintenance contact on the base, also known as "The Boss." We were joined by a maintenance technician who spoke fluent English. He would act as a translator for us.

We were led into a glassed in office that contained wooden bookcases which encircled the room. The bookcases were filled with one foot square leather suitcases. The Boss pulled down eight of the leather suitcases and placed them on a large wooden table in the middle of the room. Each of the suitcases were carefully opened and one by one, logbooks were removed and opened for our inspection.

The Boss was quick to show us the last page of each engine logbook as the final entry was an approval from MiG engineers to extend the engine life of the RD-33 jet engines. The English speaking associate said, "The RD-33 engine has a normal useful life of 350 hours before overhaul. The MiG inspection and extension took the life to 450 hours."

Tom and I spent the next hour perusing log books for the Airframe, Engines and auxiliary power units as the English translator helped clarify our questions with The Boss. Charlie stood in the back of the room and did not say anything. He just watched.

We were told that the logbooks for the seats and other weapons systems were in storage at another base approximately 300 miles away. "Would you like to drive to see them," said the translator.

Fortunately, my client had no interest in weapons, so we passed on the offer to make a 600 mile roundtrip drive and told the translator we were pleased with the logs and ready to look at planes.

From the maintenance hangar we went to inspect the aircraft with the senior maintenance technician and translator leading us in a military truck back through the base, and toward an area that looked like rolling hills. There were no MiGs, or any other aircraft in sight.

We followed the truck around the corner of a large dirt hill and there sat a Russian MiG 23 "Flogger" jet that had seen better days. The wings of the jet were folded back into the fuselage, the canopy was broken, and the tires were flat from sitting for what looked like a long, long time. I hoped that the jet was not setting an expectation for the MiG 29 we were about to inspect.

We drove past the Flogger and made a sharp right turn into a bunker. There it was, a magnificent MiG 29, and not in the sad shape that the Flogger was in. Instead, it looked like it was staged in the ready position to depart on a mission at any minute. It looked perfect.

Eight men were standing around the MiG 29 and they all snapped to attention when the chief assistant and senior maintenance technician got out of their vehicles. Within minutes of being given direction, the eight men began to remove panels from the MiG for our inspection.

Compressed air was soon applied by an external cart allowing the large canopy to be raised on its own.

All of the engine inlet and outlet covers were removed, along with access panels that helped us to visibly inspect for any damage or corrosion.

The airframe was in overall good condition showing no visible signs of damage or corrosion. All control surfaces were in good condition.

The landing gear and gear doors of the aircraft were in good condition. The brakes and tires needed to be replaced from sitting out in the elements, but the wheels were in good condition showing no signs of damage. There were no visible fluid leaks, a really good sign.

A ladder was placed by the crew to the cockpit and our translator said, "Climb on in," as he motioned to the ladder. "Careful of the explosive seats!" he added.

I climbed into the cockpit of the MiG and gently sat myself into the seat as I held onto the front canopy. The translator followed me up the ladder and began to point out systems of the jet. He reached down into the cockpit and pulled a hand brake that sent air to the brake system. "See, it works!" he said.

The translator continued to show me the features of the jet, and after just a minute or two said, "We will now start."

"Whoa," I replied. "I don't know how."

"No, you get out now. I start," he said.

I gently pulled myself out of the ejection seat by grabbing the front canopy and climbed back onto the ladder as the translator moved to the wing of the plane. Once I was down the ladder, he jumped onto the ejection seat with force, unlike my feather-like fear that it would somehow go off. "Was kidding," said the translator. "Pyro has been removed."

I could hear the switches that were flipped into position by the translator, who looked down to the others nearby on the ground, motioning that the engine was about to spin up for start. A thumbs-up was returned by the group as the Auxiliary Power Unit (APU) of the MiG came to life. I could see the flashing of warning lights in the cockpit as the translator took his right index figure and made a circle in the air that the engines were about to start.

Air from the APU was directed to engine number one of the MiG 29 and it began to spin. At the right moment, fuel and ignition were added to the spinning engine and it came to life. Air from the APU was redirected to engine number two, and like engine one, it quickly came to life as fuel and ignition were added in the start-up process.

The engines shook the earth bunker where the jet was parked. It was deafening, even though I had my fingers tightly in my ears.

The translator looked at me for approval after he extinguished the flashing warning lights. I quickly removed my finger from my right ear and gave a thumbs-up in approval.

The engines were shut down after only a minute of running.

"We must conserve fuel," said the translator as the engines came to a stop and the technicians began to look for leaks on the plane. "We have no budget for fuel," said the translator as he climbed down the MiG.

The jet had performed beyond my expectations, and I thought about how pleased my client would be after his years of searching for a worthy example. No one, until now, had found a suitable example of the MiG 29. I was sure that we would complete a sale because of the quality of the plane, and I was thrilled that I would be a part of an effort to get a flying MiG 29 into the skies of the United States.

As the maintenance team put the inspection panels back onto the jet, we were escorted back to our car by the translator, The Boss, and the chief as they debriefed in their native Romanian language.

"The Boss and the chief want to know what you think?" asked the translator. "Are you ready to buy today?"

Tom looked at me for an answer. Charlie remained quiet as he had all day.

"We need some time to look over the information," I replied.

"The commander needs an answer today," said the translator. "He will cut the price if you buy."

There was no way I could make any kind of commitment to the purchase without a firm approval from my client.

"I can't commit today," I said. "Besides, we need to inspect the rest of the spare parts before we leave."

"There will be no more inspections," responded the translator. "If you do not commit, you must leave the base," he told me, Tom and Charlie.

"Then we will have to leave," I replied, as my hopes of a sale suddenly faded.

Charlie finally said something. "I think we can get back to you with a good answer soon," he said.

The chief replied, "Then good, I will tell our commander. We will escort you to gate."

"Tell him, Thank You," said Charlie. "I will contact him with an answer."

We got into Charlie's car and made our way out of the Air Base, then traveled back to Bucharest. Charlie did not say a word the whole way back the hotel. Tom, on the other hand, pushed me the whole ride to see what I thought would happen with our client. He handed me a purchase proposal the minute we returned to Bucharest and told me that his name was on the line should there not be a deal. I couldn't answer him, but promised to try and get a purchase contract for the MiG the minute I got back to Colorado. It was a really great example of a modern fighter jet, and I hoped in my mind that our client agreed.

~~~

Despite favorable terms, and an aggressive sale price, my client passed on the MiG.

Tom asked me never to bring him any future deals. He said that the call sign he gave me, FLASH, was appropriate.

Charlie moved to Georgia and was never heard from again.

Chapter Ten

Dayton and the Wright Brothers

The board meeting had lasted over an hour longer than scheduled. New business and public comment wasn't until the end of the meeting, and I had to catch a flight. "Come on!" I said to myself, over and over, as the rambling on a topic, not even related to the purpose of the board meeting, went on and on.

It was clear to all but one of the board members at the meeting that I was anxious and wanted to speak. I was tired from a trip to Singapore the week before, I wasn't feeling good, and I was angry because I needed to say something in public comment, and now I was at risk of missing my flight to Dayton, Ohio. "Come on!" I said, just loud enough for everyone to hear. All heads turned my direction.

"Do you have something you need to say?" said the lady that was rambling on and on.

"Yes I do!" I replied, standing up.

"Well?" she said.

"You know what I am here for, and you have been stalling." I looked down at my watch and realized I had about 30 seconds before I had to leave to catch my flight, a flight that I was *not* going to miss. "You have been telling people that the Warbird book I wrote is a lie, and I am here to put an end to your rumors," I said.

"Well, it's just not possible that you went through that in Russia, and as the president of this board I say that nobody should buy your book," she said in a nasty tone.

"You weren't there," I said looking at my watch. My blood pressure was rising, along with my anger.

"Well, I know more about travel than you," she quipped. "There is no way that what you said in that book is true," she added.

"Wait a minute," said one of the other board members. "I worked in Russia around the time Gordon said he was there." "It *was* the Wild West, and exactly what he said in his book."

"Well, I don't believe it, and the board should support me on publically denouncing the book. All in favor?" she said while putting her hand in the air and looking around at the others.

Not a single other hand went up.

"You're nothing but a bully," I said as I turned around and headed to the door to catch my flight. My blood was boiling. "If I miss this flight, so help me…," I said under my breath as I got to my car. I had said what I needed to say before heading off to the National Warbird Operators Conference in Dayton, Ohio, an event where I would be selling my book.

For weeks I had heard about the negative comments and denouncement of a book I had spent the last three years writing, and the only way to contact the culprit was during public comment of the board meeting she oversaw. Having said my piece, it was time to focus on something I had wanted to see all of my life- Dayton, Ohio, and the Wright Brothers landmarks.

~~~

The flight to Dayton took me through Chicago O'Hare airport for a tight connection. The whole way to Chicago I replayed the board meeting in my head, wondering if it had been worth my time to have risked missing my flight. My energy was sapped by the time I got off the plane in Chicago, and in my head I connected the loss of energy to the adrenaline I had spent at the meeting.

We arrived at Terminal A. My connecting flight was in Terminal B in 20 minutes. I had to run in the long, underground tunnel between the two terminals in order to catch the plane to Dayton. I normally love the underground tunnel, with its George Gershwin, *Rhapsody in Blue* music playing from speakers that were hidden in the flashing neon lights that entertain millions of passengers that travel through O'Hare Airport. But today, I hated the tunnel. The moving walkways were closed for maintenance, which meant I had to run without assistance on the hard concrete.

My heart was racing as I made it to the gate of my connecting flight, just as they were about to close the doors. I took my seat for the flight to Dayton and thought to myself "I'm not feeling too hot." I felt like I was coming down with a cold. "It was probably the run," I told myself as I pulled the shade and closed my eyes.

~~~

The screeching of the main wheels of our plane woke me up from a deep sleep.

"Welcome to Dayton, please remain seated as we come to a complete stop," came from the tiny loud speaker above my seat. I had made it to the town where aviation began, but as I gathered my items in preparation to get off the plane, I felt worse than when I had left Chicago. "Why now?" I said to myself. I wanted to be on my game at the conference, sell lots of books, and see the Birthplace of Aviation. Being sick was not in my plans.

~~~

I arrived at the Dayton Marriott Hotel where I checked in and was immediately greeted in the lobby by a group of Warbird pilots. They all had drinks in hand and were of course, talking about planes. One of the pilots was Jim McKinstry, a friend of mine from Denver who owned a WWII Yak 3 fighter. I had known Jim from United Airlines Flight Training Center, who used our flight simulation software for training their pilots. Jim approached me with a beer in his hand and said, "Grab one, and join the party."

"I would, but man, I don't feel too hot," I said. "Think I'll go to bed early and see you guys tomorrow."

"Well, don't be late. We're going to the state park to see the Wright Flyer," Jim said. He finished his sentence by taking a drink from his beer.

"Don't worry, I'll be there. No way I'm going to miss any landmarks," I said as I grabbed my bag and headed to the elevator.

I got to my room and immediately pulled some Alka-Seltzer cold medicine from my bag. I mixed it with water, drank it and headed to bed with the hope that I would awake cold free.

~~~

The next morning came fast, and I felt even worse than the night before. The Alka-Seltzer hadn't worked. I had no energy, but unlike having a cold or flu, I had no runny nose or fever. I took another Alka-Seltzer and then drank a pot of coffee in the room before heading down to the conference. "Come on!" I said in anger as I grabbed a stack of books and made my way to the door. No time for this! I thought with little hope that I would be feeling anything like myself that day.

~~~

Jim McKinstry had saved me a seat in the conference room and motioned to me to come sit with him.

"You don't look so good," he said. "Did you have a few last night after I saw you?" he added.

"Hardly," I said. "Went right to bed." I sat down next to Jim for the opening session of the conference, which happened to be medical issues for pilots.

The day went by fast as session after session was presented to the room full of pilots. Then it was time for the afternoon tour, a one mile walk from the hotel to Carillon Historic Park to see the original 1905 Wright Flyer III.

I had looked forward to this part of the conference, along with the other tours to see the Wright Brothers Cycle Shop, and the National Museum of the United States Air Force. All sites were high on my list of places I wanted to see.

I joined up with Jim McKinstry for the walk to the park.

"You still don't look good," he said as we started walking down a narrow sidewalk.

"I feel like I have the flu, but no real symptoms," I said.

"Did you hear about Dan?" Jim said. "You know, the guy that has been working on my Yak."

"No, what about him."

"He wasn't feeling too good last week, went to the doctor, and the next thing you know- quadruple bypass," Jim said. "Doing okay now, but my Yak won't be ready for Reno."

"Uh, bummer," I replied, equating what he said to how I felt. "Glad he is okay," I added as we continued walking.

My mind started to play tricks on me, as I thought about another friend who had also just had heart surgery. Two? I thought to myself. What's going on?

We completed the mile walk and I couldn't quit thinking about Dan and my other friend as I was starting to struggle breathing. Anxiety set in as we entered the building where the Wright Flyer was on display. I barely looked at the plane before telling Jim, "I'm going to walk back to the hotel, and then run to Urgent Care to see if I can get some medicine."

"But we just got here," said Jim.

"I know, but I am really not feeling well."

"Remember we have the big dinner and tour at the museum tonight," Jim said. "Hope to see you there."

~~~

I made the one mile walk back to the hotel and asked the front desk attendant if there was an Urgent Care facility in the area.

"Yeah, just down the street," he said as he pulled out a map and began to draw lines on it. "You don't look too well," he said.

"I don't feel too hot," I added.

"Well, definitely go get some help. The last guy who went to Urgent Care from here ended up with a bypass. He was just 32," said the attendant as he handed me the map.

"What the hell?" I said, as I took the map and headed to my rental car.

~~~

The Urgent Care facility was a mile from the Marriott. There were only a few patients in the lobby as I checked in. I was asked to fill out a questionnaire about my problem. I handed the completed form to the receptionist, who reviewed it and then asked me a few questions. "Based on what you are saying, we are going to send you next door," said the receptionist.

"What's next door?" I said.

"The Dayton Heart Hospital."

~~~

All I could think about as I entered the reception of the adjoining building was what Jim had said about Dan. *How could this happen to me?* I asked myself. *I run, workout, eat somewhat okay. What did I do wrong?*

It wasn't long after I checked in, that I was escorted to a room that contained three hospital beds that were only separated by a thin curtain hung from the ceiling. There was an elderly gentlemen in the bed nearest the door who was being attended to. I was led to the farthest bed, leaving an empty bed between me and the elderly fellow. I was told to undress and get into a hospital gown.

I was scared. I didn't have my cell phone, didn't have my stuff from the hotel, didn't have a way to contact Jim or anyone from the conference, or worse, my wife.

A female nurse came into the room after I had put on the skimpy gown and took my vitals. "The Doctor will be in, in just a minute," she said after she finished filling out her forms. "Busy day here," she added.

Just then another gentleman was rolled into the room and the curtain was pulled between my bed and the one that my new roommate would be in. "Welcome back Doc," said my nurse as she exited the room.

The doctor on call entered the room and walked toward my bed. Passing my neighbor, he said "Hey Doc. Heard you were coming in."

"Yeah, fourth time, and I'm a damn coroner," said the guy in the bed next to me.

"We'll fix you up good this time," said the Doctor. He walked to my bed and greeted me as he pulled up my chart for review. "Doesn't look too bad from your vitals, but let's give you a nitro glycerin patch just in case. We're going to keep you overnight for observation and do some blood work. But it doesn't look serious, like Doc next door," he said. "We'll do an EKG in a bit."

The nurse returned for a blood draw and placed a gooey patch on my arm. "This will slow you down," she said as she applied the nitro glycerin patch. "Try to get some rest," she added. "I have to do your blood work about every two hours, so it will be a long night."

"Hey Doc," she said as she moved from my bed to my roommate's.

I closed my eyes, said a prayer, and hoped to God that I was going to be okay.

Not long after the blood draw, I was given an EKG that did not show any signs of a problem. That was somewhat reassuring for the moment.

~~~

It was indeed a long night. I tried to sleep when I could and prayed when I couldn't.

The elderly gentleman who was in the room when I first arrived had died during the night from a massive heart attack. Doc had survived the night and was harassing the nurse the next morning. The situation was not worrisome to him, but I was still scared.

A new nurse came to my bed and told me that the blood work that was taken during the night was not showing any signs of problems. "The morning doctor would like to do another EKG," she said. "He will be in soon."

It wasn't five minutes later that I was hooked up by the morning nurse to once again have an EKG test. A new doctor introduced himself as he entered my room and began to run the test. "I see you are from Colorado and the nurse says you're a pilot," he said. "I have a place in Vail. You ever been there?" he asked as he stared at the machine. "Sure, I am skier," I said. "Mostly ski-erd to be here," I added in a voice that was a bad impression of a comedy skit by Jose Jimenez from the '70s.

"Ha, I remember that skit," said the doctor, as he more closely looked at the machine.

"I'm not saying you have a problem, but I would like to do an angiogram just to make sure," said the doctor. "I'll be puttin' a stint in 'ole Doc this morning anyway, so no problem to check you out at the same time."

I started to shake from fear. Quadruple bypass was all I could think about. "It'll be okay," said the doctor. "You want to do it?"

After a more detailed explanation from the doctor, I reluctantly agreed to do the procedure. "Just a snip in the groin area, run the camera to the heart, do what we have to, if anything." "We can have you out later today if all goes well," the doctor explained. "We'll start in about an hour," he added.

The next hour was the most stressful hour of my life. I had come to Dayton to see some Wright Brothers landmarks. Not, what was about to happen...

~~~

"Hey, the doc said that you're a pilot," said a husky male ER nurse as I lay on the table for the Angiogram. "You can watch the procedure on that monitor," he said.

"I'll pass," I replied.

"What brings you to Dayton," said the nurse, as the doctor entered the room in full surgical gear.

"Here for a Warbird conference, but to see the Wright Brother sites too. Something I really wanted to do instead of this," I said. "Not going to happen this trip," I added.

The big guy pulled up the sleeve on his scrubs to expose a giant tattoo of the Wright Flyer on his right bicep. "How you like this?" he said.

"It is probably the closest I will get to a Wright Brothers item this trip," I said as a sedative started to kick in.

~~~

"All done," said the doctor as I awakened. The procedure was over and I didn't remember a thing. I cautiously lifted my left arm to touch my chest to make sure I hadn't had open heart surgery. I hadn't! However, my right groin area was achy. "You have lots of wind going to your sails," said the doctor. "All good," he added.

"So what is going on?" I asked.

"You might have a virus," he said. "Do you travel much?"

"Just got back from Singapore," I said.

"There's something on the news today about a virus going around that masks heart issues. You just might have that, but better safe than sorry," said the doctor, as he pulled down his mask and began to clean up. "We'll get you out of here soon."

~~~

I picked up my bags, along with a stack of books I never got to sell from the front desk of the hotel, just in time to turn around and head to the airport for my flight back to Denver. I had missed the entire conference, a private dinner and tour of the National Museum of the United States Air Force, and sadly, the Wright Brothers Cycle Shop. What a trip...

Jim McKinstry was at the United Airlines gate for the flight to Denver as I arrived. I was walking with a limp from the angiogram. "What the hell happened to you?" Jim said. "You had us all scared to death, and, you missed all the good stuff," he added.

"Well, sometimes reality gets in the way of a plan," I said as we boarded the plane.

Three months later...

I was the co-pilot on the B-25 that Rob Collings and I were taking to Zanesville, Ohio for two days of passenger flights. The air was smooth, visibility unlimited, with two radial engines lumping along while Rob and I made small talk over our headsets.

"Hey, look down, were going over Dayton," he said. "Ever been there? I love the history."

I let out a long, deep sigh.

"Not my favorite place, Rob," I replied.

"Let me tell you a story..."

Chapter Eleven

The Albatross and the Snake

Falcon Field in Mesa, Arizona has always been a favorite destination of mine, especially in the winter. It is a treasure trove of aviation history with the Commemorative Air Force, Arizona Wing as the centerpiece. On the east side of the airfield sits Marsh Aviation, which since the early 1960s has been engineering and modifying aircraft for customers around the globe. They are experts in anything built by Grumman Aircraft.

I stood in the parking lot of Marsh Aircraft on an early spring day admiring a Grumman S-2 Tracker that was in pieces. As I was standing there, thinking about the day I would own one of the twin-engine, sub-hunters, the small door to the office opened and an elderly women yelled at me.

"You can't take pictures of that!" she said

"Not taking any pictures, just admiring," I said.

"Well, get away from there. What do you want?" she added.

"I'm here to inspect some Grumman Albatross planes," I replied.

"Yeah, the owner's inside waiting for you. Come on in."

In the small doorway to the office, still decorated from the '60's, stood a guy with a paper coffee cup in one hand. He was shoving a handful of popcorn in his mouth with the other. He wiped his hand off on the front of his shirt and stuck it out to shake my hand.

"Hey, thanks for coming," he said. "Gotta get this all done today. I am back to Illinois early tomorrow. Follow me," he said, as the lady who had yelled at me earlier sat down in front of a computer monitor. "Out this way."

I followed him out a small side door, through a graveyard of aircraft parts and engines, then out to the concrete ramp to the side of the main building.

There sat a faded Grumman G-111 Albatross with massive oil puddles under each engine. Its propellers were missing. The old bird had spent a lot of time in the Arizona sun and sat in a way that cried, "Please pay some attention to me."

The Albatross was overall white, with some visible streaks of surface rust from water leaking from the high wing onto the fuselage. Painted in light blue paint on the front of the fuselage were the words "CHALK'S." "CHALK'S" was also painted on the massive vertical stabilizer.

"There it is," said the owner. "Good luck," he added.

"I only see one," I said. "I thought we were going to look at a total of ten planes."

"We are," he replied.

"The rest are in Tucson. That's why you gotta hustle," he said.

"Isn't that a few hours away?" I said.

"No problem. Just about three hours, round trip," he replied. "Gotta make some calls, so climb on up there and get going," he added.

I turned to the massive seaplane and shook my head. It was going to be a *long* day.

~~~

As I began my inspection of the Albatross, I thought about its flying history.

At one time, the plane was owned by Merv Griffin's Resorts International, who had 13 Grumman Albatrosses converted from Experimental HU-16 versions to Standard category as G-111s. The conversion made them eligible to be used in scheduled airline operations from Florida to the Bahamas.

These aircraft had extensive modification from the standard military configuration, including rebuilt wings with titanium wing spar caps, additional doors and modifications to existing doors and hatches, stainless steel engine oil tanks, dual engine fire extinguishing systems on each engine, and propeller auto feather systems installed.

The G-111s were only operated for a few years by Resorts International, and then put in storage in Arizona.

As the owner took out his cell phone to make calls he told me that the plane I was inspecting was scheduled to be converted to a turbine powered aircraft, but it had sat in front of Marsh Aircraft for years, waiting for someone to spend the money to do the conversion.

I climbed inside and out of the Albatross, documenting the good and the bad. For an airplane that had only been in service for three years, salt water had taken a toll. It had seen better days.

I spent the next hour inspecting and photographing the Albatross. It was obvious that the plane had spent a lot of time in the water as there was visible corrosion. It was especially noticeable on the tops of the wings.

As I stood on the tops of the wings, looking at the corrosion, the owner yelled at me. "Hurry up!" "We gotta go," he said.

I snapped a few final photographs and climbed down and out of the plane.

"Let's go. Follow me," he said, as we walked out to our cars. "Stay close so I can get you through security," he added. "You won't be able to get through the gate without me."

We climbed into our cars and left the Marsh parking lot. I could see the owner eating some more popcorn from a big bag he had in his car. He was alternating eating handfuls of popcorn with swigs from a huge bottle of soda.

I was hungry and thirsty after all of the climbing around the plane and had not planned for an hour and a half drive. I hoped for the chance to stop by a gas station for some refreshments, but that was not to be.

The owner drove the entire hour and a half with the only stop being at the guard shack at the Pinal Airpark Airport near Marana, Arizona.

I was waved through the gate and stayed close to the owner's car as we passed rows of mothballed airliner jets that were sitting in storage in the dry Arizona climate.

We passed a Boeing 747 that we emblazed with EVERGREEN on the side of it. I had read about the 747 just a day before. It was being converted into a fire fighting plane and was having an engine changed on it as we passed by.

We passed by a row of Beech Starships, that were mothballed by Raytheon after sales of the radically designed pusher-type plane never took off (no pun intended).

Rounding a corner, the nine other Grumman Albatross aircraft sat in the hot summer sun of Arizona. I parked next to the owner's car and got out as a small pickup pulled up next to us.

"This is Mike," said the owner, as he pulled another handful of popcorn from the bag and shoved it in his mouth. "Sorry, I should have offered you some," he said as he took the big bag and turned it over, shaking out some small crumbs to the ground.

"Mike will unlock the planes for you to look at them," he said. "Have at it. I'm going to make some calls while you do your thing."

"Follow me," said Mike. "Also, watch out. Its snake season, and they just came out." "They are exceptionally aggressive this year," had added.

Just great, I thought to myself.

I admit that I have three Kryptonite's. Snakes, needles and Brussels sprouts. I have gone my entire life hearing that snakes aren't that bad. They scare me to death.

I have also heard, "Well if you had Brussels sprouts the way I fixed them, you would like them." No, no I won't. As President George H.W. Bush said, "Not gonna do it."

Mike opened up the first Albatross. "Man, I really hope that these don't get scrapped," he said. "Heard that is an option."

"They need to get back in the air," he added as he motioned for me to enter the plane. "Just let me know if you need anything."

I began the first inspection with the same hope that the planes would not get scrapped.

I spent the next three hours in the hot sun looking at each of the Grumman seaplanes, taking photos and making notes, and hoping to God that I would not accidently step on a snake.

The planes were mostly in the same condition as the one I had looked at in Mesa, but several had maintenance done on them in the hopes that they would soon have new owners who would put them back in the sky, and on the water.

It was indeed, a long day.

I completed my inspections and walked back to the car feeling heat exhaustion, but thankful that I had not seen a rattle snake. The owner completed a call he was on and took a final swig of his giant soda.

"Well?" "Did you get what you need?" he said as Mike locked up the planes in the background.

"Yes I did," I replied.

"Good, because we need your report to make a decision on what to do next," he said.

"Well, I hope that these birds can fly again, or at least make it into a museum or two," I said.

"Not sure, but I gotta go," said the owner as he got in his car and started the engine. He grabbed a big bag of Doritos and opened them as he drove away.

Mike walked over to me as I was about to get into the car. "You see the six footer?"

"What?" I replied. "A six foot snake?"

"Yeah, it's right over there where you were walking," he said as he pointed toward the third plane I had looked at.

"Nice to have met you, but I'm out of here," I said, as I slammed the door and started the engine. I might as well have seen the snake, because I thought of it the entire hour and a half drive back to Phoenix, and never made any stops.

I had done my part to hopefully save some history, but had zero desire to see a seaplane in the desert again.

~~~

Four years later...

I was standing in front of a Grumman Albatross at Universal Studios in Orlando, Florida. It belonged to singer Jimmy Buffett, and was part of an outdoor bar in a busy area of the City Walk at Universal.

"Hey, did you see the bullet hole?" said a guy with a British accent.

He pointed to an area on the forward fuselage that had an obvious patch.

"I have heard about it," I replied. "First time to see it."

"Ever been in one of those planes?" asked the Brit.

I thought about the Arizona desert, and a near miss with a snake, then answered.

"Why yes, yes I have."

Chapter Twelve

The Parts Trip

"Hey, it's Maj. Come get your shiiii…, I mean stuff. I need the room," was all that was on the voicemail on my cell phone.

Maj was the owner of Fighting Classics, in Marana, Arizona, and a master builder of the Douglas A-4 Skyhawk. His shop was busy with restorations of several A-4s when he kindly took time out from his projects to run to Phoenix for me to pick up some parts that were destined to come to our museum in Colorado. I had promised Maj that I would be down in a rental truck to pick up the parts soon. That was a year ago.

I put a plan together where I would fly to Tucson, pick up a 16' rental truck, drive it to Marana to pick up the parts, then back to Denver. Maj would be off my back.

I didn't want to do the drive by myself, so a convinced a friend to come along for an adventure. My friend, Jon, had bugged me for years to be a part of a recovery project, so I contacted him in hopes that he would help with the loading of the parts, along with some driving duty. Jon agreed to come along, but could only take three days out of a construction project he oversaw. So I arranged a one-way flight for the two of us, and then secured a reservation of a rental truck near the Tucson airport.

I made a call to let Maj know the plan.

"Hey Maj, good news," I said as he answered the phone. 'Coming to get the parts, day after tomorrow."

"I was going to call you, Dude," he said. "There's a guy in Houston wanting to trade you some parts you've been looking for. Said he wants some of the stuff down here. Said he would pay the shipping cost too," he added.

I thought to myself about a slight detour back to Denver to get some WWII parts I wanted, but to get some extra money for the trip. "I'll do it," I told Maj. "You let him know we'll have the stuff there in three days."

"Great, plus I need the room," replied Maj. "See you soon."

I called Jon after I hung up with Maj to let him know about our detour to Houston.

"Houston! I've only got three days!" was the response I got from Jon when I told him about the change of plans.

"Come on, it's not that far out of the way, especially if we take turns driving," I said, hoping Jon would not bail on our trip.

"Okay, but I'm going to push you to get back on time," Jon replied.

We had a deal, and besides, 2300 miles in three days didn't sound all *that* bad.

~~~

Jon and I arrived in Tucson after an uneventful flight on a United Express CRJ-200.

A quick taxi ride got us to the rental facility where a lone 16' moving truck sat in a parking lot. The rental truck was the worst example of any kind of rental I had ever seen, having looked like it had been in war zone. There were multiple dents in the box of the truck, where renters had run into walls and more. The tires were worn nearly to the core, and the windshield was broken. I couldn't believe that it was safe enough to drive, let alone rent.

"Are you the guys renting our truck today?" asked the agent as we entered the small office.

"We're supposed to rent a truck, but is the one out front *the truck*?" I said,

"All we got, man," he said. "It'll get you to Denver. That's where you're going, right?"

"Yeah, eventually," I replied.

"You got your driver's license and credit card so we can get you on the road?" he asked.

I pulled the items out of me wallet while Jon blankly starred out the front window at the truck. "We're really going to do this?" he asked.

"Don't worry. Piece of cake," I answered, as I signed the rental documents.

The agent slid a key to me with a huge plastic tag on it. The tag said, "Bring it back clean or pay deposit."

"I take it that the last guy paid the deposit," I said to the agent, as I grabbed the key and headed out the door. Jon followed along.

"Jump in. Let's get to Maj's, load up in an hour and head to Texas," I said to Jon.

"Nice windshield," said Jon, as he jumped into the passenger side of the cab.

~~~

The automatic transmission on the truck stayed in low gear, despite being in the drive position. Just as I was about to turn around to take it back, it lurched into drive and we were soon merging onto Interstate 10, toward Marana, Arizona.

The 24 mile drive was not a good indicator of how the trip ahead was to go. The transmission did the low gear lurch every time we accelerated from a stop, and the windshield whistled on the passenger side of the cab.

"We'll look at that when we get to Maj's," I promised Jon.

~~~

We made it to Fighting Classics, where Maj was waiting outside of the open hangar door for us.

"That's the truck your taking all your shit in?" he said, after I had shut off the engine and had opened the creaky driver's door to get out.

"Nice to see you too," I said to Maj, as we exchanged a bro hug.

"Seriously, that things not near big enough. Look at the containers," he said as he pointed to four large wooden crates which were 4' by 4' by 8'. "And don't forget the engine on the stand," he added, pointing toward a jet engine on a steel stand that was about 12' in length.

There was no way that we could get the crates and the engine into the cargo box of the truck.

"You might be able to take the tires out of the crates to make some room," said Maj.

After some quick measuring in my head, I agreed with Maj, while Jon looked on before saying, "So much for getting out of here fast."

Two hours later, Jon and I, with Maj's help, had loaded over 200 tires, the jet engine, a canopy, and some fuel tanks and were ready to head back on the road.

"Hey, what about the rest of it?" said Maj. He pointed to another wooden crate in the storage yard. "That's yours too."

"Maj, is there any way…," I said before being interrupted.

"Dude!" said Maj. "Just get outta here," he added. "See you in another year."

"No, really…," I replied.

"Yeah, yeah, just go and have a safe trip," Maj said, waiving us off with both hands in the air.

~~~

Our 2300 mile drive began with the truck transmission staying in low gear again, this time for nearly five miles before it lurched into drive.

"Should we stop and try to get another truck?" I asked Jon as we merged back onto I-10.

"Hell no!" he said. "No way that I'm unloading those tires until we get back to Denver."

The windshield began to whistle as Jon just shook his head.

~~~

Our first fuel stop was at a truck stop in Willcox, Arizona. The whistling of the windshield was driving Jon mad, but I had a plan.

As Jon pumped gas into the truck, I purchased a roll of duct tape from the cashier. I ran a strip of the tape around the edges of the windshield and assured Jon there would be no more whistling the rest of the trip. Jon finished pumping gas and put the nozzle on the pump, then ran to the driver's side of the cab.

"You test it," he said, motioning me to get into the passenger seat.

~~~

I was glad that Jon wanted to drive, as the truck stayed in low gear up a three mile hill as we departed Willcox. After 15 grueling minutes in low gear, the rental truck kicked into drive. As we got to a normal cruise speed, the windshield began to whistle again, but this time on the driver's side of the cab.

"Think I'll take a nap," I said, as Jon clinched his teeth and grunted in disgust.

Before I could close my eyes we passed a sign that said, "WELCOME TO TEXAS."

"I've never been here," Jon said. "Is this what Texas looks like?" he asked as we drove through the desert.

My Texas experiences had mostly been in Dallas, San Antonio and Houston, not the rural West side.

"Yeah, pretty much," I replied. "Don't expect pine trees and deer like in Colorado."

We had a plan to drive to San Antonio for the night, but still had nearly 12 hours to go.

~~~

The whine of the truck engine woke me from a deep sleep. It was dark outside and we Jon was driving us up a steep incline.

"Bout' time you woke up," Jon said. "Damn thing just kicked down, and it was doing so well!"

"Thought you said there weren't any pine trees in Texas?" he said.

"Who knew?" I answered.

The truck continued up the mountain in painful fashion.

"This thing sucks!" I said.

Jon petted the dash, and said, "Don't' listen. Just get us to Colorado, Honey. Talk to her nice!" he demanded.

He was right. We had to take care of the truck, so it would take care of us.

I petted the dash and asked for forgiveness. Just then the truck lurched into drive gear.

"See?" said Jon.

No comment, I thought to myself.

~~~

We continued driving until after midnight, and we were still hours from San Antonio.

"I can't take it no more," I said to Jon.

"Cranky, I see," he replied as he grabbed the wheel of the truck and pulled himself back and forth in a motion to keep on going.

"We gotta stop for the night, Jon. Pull off at the next exit that has a hotel."

Ten miles later we pulled off on an exit and into the parking lot of a small Alpine-style motel. The lot was full of cars, but no lights were on in the hotel lobby. The door was locked when we tried to enter the lobby. A small handwritten sign was taped to the door that said, "CALL OFFICE FOR A ROOM." A phone number was scribbled on the sign that I immediately called. We hoped we could get a room to take the edge off a long day of driving.

I could hear a phone ringing at the receptionist desk I was staring at through the lobby window.

Lights came on and from around the corner came an old lady with her hair up in curlers. She unlocked the front door. "What do ya want?" she said before opening the door.

"Need a room for a few hours," I replied.

"We don't rent rooms for that," she said, then looked at Jon.

"No, not that," I replied. "Driving that truck over there and need a few good hours of sleep."

"One hundred for the room," she said as she opened the door to let us in.

It was literally highway robbery, but I needed to sleep, so I pulled out my credit card.

"Sorry, cash only this late."

I handed the old lady all of the cash I had for the trip. She in turn, handed me a key that was attached to a sawed-off broom handle with the number THREE engraved on it. It looked like the key to a gas station bathroom.

"Checkout is at noon," said the old lady, as she walked us to the door and locked it behind us. She walked around the corner and the lights were turned off in an instant.

Jon and I went to room three and not to our surprise it was a dump. It looked like it may have been used earlier that night. We were too tired to care and immediately got into a much used, and lumpy bed for a few hours of sleep.

"Let's get on the road at 5AM to keep up with our schedule," Jon said as he set an alarm on his phone.

"Ugh… Night," I said before instantly falling asleep.

~~~

"Deer! Deer!" said Jon to awake me from what seemed like a 10 minute combat nap.

"Thought you said they weren't in Texas, sleepyhead," he asked. "Time to get going, just two days to go," he added as he looked out the window at two deer that were walking around the parking lot.

"I know, I know," I said as I dragged myself out of the lumpy bed, trying to wake up for a long day of driving.

~~~

"Come on Bessy," I begged, as I was driving up a steep incline just outside of the motel.

The rental truck was in first gear again, and the engine was wound up like a top fuel dragster on a quarter mile run, only we were doing just 15 miles per hour.

"Treat her nice, G," said Jon. "Remember, she…"

"Yes, I know," I replied as I prayed that the engine would not blow up.

Jon reminded me, "Just two hours to San Antonio from here."

~~~

After a solid fifteen minutes in first gear, the truck finally went into drive. "We're on our way," said Jon. "I wonder if there is some kind of governor on this thing for weight," he added.

I didn't say a word, instead focusing on my plan to get to San Antonio, then on Houston. We had to get to Ellington Field in Houston, unload some tires and parts in a hurry to get back on the road to Dallas for a date with a steakhouse I had promised to Jon.

~~~

Ole Bessy stayed in drive and did a great job for the drive to Houston. We had blasted through San Antonio, avoiding traffic by staying to the north. The rest of the drive to Ellington Field was smooth as could be, and we arrived at the south gate of the Ellington Airport about two hours ahead of schedule.

I could taste the steak that I would be enjoying later that night. More importantly, I was looking forward to getting a full night of sleep before the last stretch of the drive home.

Inside of the south gate to the airport sat a Russian MiG 21 fighter jet. There was an external starting cart next to the jet, and two men, dressed in flight suits, were inspecting the plane for what looked like a flight.

As I watched the pre-flight on the MiG from the south gate, I called the cell phone of the guy I was supposed to meet to do the parts swap.

"Hey, it's Rick," answered the guy on the other end of the call.

"It's Gordon and we are here at the south gate."

One of the guys in a flight suit walked around the MiG 21 with a cell phone in hand. He waved at the truck.

"That you in that beater truck," he asked.

"Yeah. Can you let us in," I replied.

"Be right there, but we're about to go burn some JET A, so you will have to wait around a bit," Rick said as he hung up and stuffed the phone in the top pocket of his flight suit.

Rick walked to the gate, punched in a code to open it, and soon we had driven through.

"Hey, good to meet you guys, but we are going flying. Stick around and watch what this thing will do," said Rick as the gate closed behind us.

Jon and I drove the rental truck past the side of a hangar and into an open field near where the MiG was parked. The exhaust of the Cold War jet was pointed toward the grass in the field.

Rick and his passenger climbed into the jet as a guy providing ground support plugged in the start cart.

"Back in a bit," Rick yelled at me and Jon as we watched from a safe distance, next to the hangar.

Soon the spinning of the jet engine was underway and the ground support person unplugged the start cart.

"Kind of sounds like the rental truck in low gear," Jon said as hit put his index fingers in his ears.

Rick added power to the MiG to begin the taxi to the main runway at Ellington.

Suddenly, the grass in the field was on fire from the heat of the jet engine.

As the jet taxied past me and Jon, the ground support guy grabbed a fire extinguisher and ran to the field to put out the flames. A few squeezes on the extinguisher is all it took to put out the fire, leaving charred grass from the start of the MiG.

"Happens all the time," said the support guy, who then asked if we wanted to come with him to watch the takeoff. We agreed, and jumped into the back of his pickup for a ride to the main terminal which housed a glassed in viewing area.

~~~

The afterburner of the MiG 21 shook the windows of the glass viewing area as the jet roared down the runway into a steep climb.

"That's that," said the support guy. "He'll be back in an hour or so," he added.

"So much for a quick turn," Jon said.

He was right.

~~~

An hour later, the MiG 21 returned to the pattern of Ellington Airport. In my mind, the jet would land, quickly taxi to parking to shut down, then we could load up and get on the road. It was not to be, as the MiG made approach, after approach, to simulate a landing before going around the pattern. Rick made five such approaches, before finally landing the jet. He taxied back to the hangar, then parked in the spot where the jet had earlier set the grass on fire. The charred grass did not re-ignite, but the support guy had an extinguisher in hand, just in case.

Rick opened the canopy of the MiG as the engine spooled to a stop.

"Just give us a minute to de-brief, then we can put the jet away and then do our deal," he said.

~~~

Rick's debrief lasted an hour and a half. After that he emerged from the hangar and asked for help putting the jet away. That took another hour. I thought we were finally ready to do the parts swap and asked Rick if he was ready.

"Sure am," he said, as I started toward the back of the rental truck.

"Oh. The parts aren't here," said Rick. "They're across town." "Just follow me," he said as he walked over and opened a car door.

"Well just shit," I told Jon. "A steak dinner in Dallas is fading."

~~~

We drove across Houston in what was now rush hour traffic. It took nearly an hour to get to a rundown storage facility, where Rick led us to a roll up door in the middle area of the units. We got out of the truck as Rick shut his car door.

"Well, here it is. Let's start unloading," said Rick as he rolled up the door to a unit that was filled with parts from floor to ceiling. "Let's put those tires in the back."

Jon looked at me in disgust as I walked to the back of the truck and opened the door to expose the parts and tires we had loaded in Arizona.

It took another hour to unload the tires and parts as darkness was settling on day two.

When we are done with the parts swap, Rick said, "You boys look hungry, let's grab some dinner."

"That steak isn't going to happen," Jon said. "Let's just eat here and get back on the road."

Two hours later, after eating some lousy Mexican food, Jon and I were finally back on the road. The parts swap with Rick was complete, but instead of being ahead of our travel schedule, we were now six hours behind. Jon reminded me that he *had* to be home the next day as we set out for Dallas. Instead of steak and a good night of sleep, we would have to drive until at least 3AM to stay on schedule.

~~~

"Mr. Cranky Pants," Jon said as I begged him to pull over in Amarillo, Texas to spend the night. The only thing of interest from the previous nine and a half hours of driving had been seeing a giant stone statue of Sam Houston, and a roadside sign that reminded those driving by to visit "Old Sparky," an electric chair at the Texas State Prison that had executed 361 prisoners before being decommissioned.

The sign brought a morbid chuckle as we drove by, thanks to my mother-in-law, Carol Mills, who had nicknamed the stair chair she used to get her up and down the stairs in her house, "Old Sparky."

Jon pulled over to six different motels in Amarillo, each one with overflowing parking lots of oil field work trucks, before we gave up and continued driving toward Colorado. An oil and gas boom in Texas had filled every hotel room from Amarillo to Dalhart. We finally found a place to crash for a few hours. We would get three desperately needed hours of sleep before getting back on the road in order to get Jon home in time.

The *only* reason I could keep on driving was thanks to Red Bull, and the driving, rockabilly music of The Reverend Horton Heat.

~~~

We crossed the Colorado state line when I received a phone call from a friend in Colorado Springs.

"Hey Gordon," it's Bill Dude. "Maj told me that you would headed by our place with some parts we could really use." "We got cash, so can you stop by?"

Looking at my watch, we only had about thirty extra minutes to do a quick stop, then get back on the road to get Jon home on time.

"Sure," I replied, without asking Jon if an extra stop would be okay with him.

"See you around three," I told Bill Dude and hung up.

"You did *not* do what I think you did!" Jon asked me with narrowed eyes. "Guess I'm not getting home in time."

"Hey, it'll only take a half hour," I said.

"That's what you said in Houston," Jon said. "Look how that worked out."

~~~

We pulled into the parking lot of a hangar at the Colorado Springs Airport where Bill Dude was waiting outside of the entrance door. "We got thirty minutes," I said as I jumped out of the driver's seat of the rental truck.

"Man, you look like shit. Kind of like that truck," said Bill Dude.

"Yeah, whatever, we gotta turn and burn to get my friend back to Denver," I said, as Jon jumped out of the truck.

An hour later, an angry Jon, and I were back on the road, heading toward Denver. I drove as fast as I could and hoping we wouldn't hit rush hour in Denver, all so I could be good on my promise to Jon.

Traffic worked in our favor and I delivered Jon to his door with five minutes to spare.

"Sorry I can't help you unload," Jon said as he grabbed his bag and opening the door of the truck. "Hope that engine isn't too much of a pain," said Jon. "See you Cranky Pants," he added as he slammed the door.

I thanked him, then started the truck to drive to the museum to unload parts and the engine. My neighbors next to the museum graciously helped unload so I could return the rental truck in time to avoid paying for an extra day. I never wanted to drive a rental truck again in my life after returning Ole Bessy.

We had made it. Three days, 2300 miles, in 32 hours of driving, but it sucked.

One year later…

My cell phone alerted me that there was a voicemail waiting. "Hey, it's Maj." "Thought you said the extra box would be outta here soon?" he asked in frustration. "Come get your shit."

Jon declined my request when I asked him to join me on another adventure.

The box is still at Maj's place.

Chapter Thirteen

Betty's Red

I have always loved the name, Betty. My Grandma Betty spoiled me as a kid, always baking treats for me and my brother and sister. My grandpa, the world's greatest teaser, was good at watching my Grandma Betty work in the kitchen while he enjoyed a glass of what I thought was Coca Cola. I once asked him for a sip, but he said, "Oh no, that's the sweetwater."

I never knew what the sweetwater was until the day of his funeral, when a bottle of Maker's Mark was passed around at the reception. "Here's to Gordon's sweetwater," was the toast that answered the question why I could never have any—until that day.

My Grandpa Gordon had always told me that Grandma was *THE* Betty Page. "You know, the pin-up model from the 1950's," he would always say. Grandma never denied the story, but always encouraged me to keep dreaming, like the way Grandpa dreamed.

I didn't hear much from my grandma and grandpa after my family moved from Missouri to Boulder, Colorado. I was just twelve when we moved, but the name Betty touched my life on the ramp of the Boulder, Colorado airport one summer day.

I had ridden my bike to the airport that day in the hopes that I could wash planes in exchange for flight time. Sadly, no one took me up on my offer, but instead of going home, I had stuck around the airport to watch any planes come and go.

As I sat on the balcony of the terminal building, a small, yellow, bi-plane made a low pass over the runway, then pulled to the sky as it was at the midpoint of the field. I had never seen a plane do something like that, and the whine of the propeller kept my eyes fixated on the plane as it banked sharply to enter the pattern to land.

"Betty's back," said an old man who was sitting in a plastic chair near me.

The small plane turned back toward the runway, then began to fly sideways as it descended to earth. "Is it going to crash?" I asked the old man.

"No, that's a slip, so she can see the runway," he replied.

The yellow plane continued to fall, but right before it was about to hit the ground, it straightened out to line up with the runway and gently touched down with a chirp of the tires. I was fascinated as the little plane taxied in front of where I was watching and shut down the engine.

"Want to meet Betty?" said the old man as he stood up from the cheap plastic chair.

I couldn't resist and followed him down the stairs and to the plane where a lady was climbing out of the bi-plane.

"How'd it go?" the old man asked as lady pulled a parachute from her back.

"I think I'm ready," she replied. "Who's this?"

"I think this kid likes your plane," he replied. "What's your name, kid?"

"Uh, Randy Page," I said.

"Meet Betty, who's about to be the best damn pilot in the world," said the old man as he pointed to the lady.

"You're not from around here, are you," said Betty. "You're accent isn't from here."

"No Ma'am, just moved here from Missouri," I replied while examining the little yellow plane.

"You like planes?" she said.

"Like 'em all, but have never seen one like this," I said as I noticed the word *PITTS Special* in a flowing script painted on the tail.

"You want to fly someday?" Betty asked.

"Yeah, I want to fly a P-51," I said.

"Keep chasing your dreams. Maybe someday," Betty said.

She threw the parachute around her shoulder and began walking toward the terminal building.

"Well, take a walk around and look at the plane, but *don't touch* anything," said Betty.

The old man walked over and joined her.

"Remember, don't touch anything!" she said as she walked away.

"Yeah, she's going to the World's," added the old man.

I inspected every inch of the plane, resisting the temptation to touch, and by the time I walked away from it, I had promised myself that someday I would have one of my own.

~~~

Forty years later…

The latest issue of EAA Sport magazine was sitting on my desk when I got into the office. Flipping through the pages, I ran across an article announcing the induction of Betty Stewart into the International Aerobatic Hall of Fame.

The article highlighted that Betty had been a member of the 1976, 1980 and 1982 United States aerobatic teams. She was honored as the first person to win the World Champion title at two consecutive world events. In 1980, she won three individual gold medals and the title Women's World Aerobatic Champion. In 1982, she repeated the feat winning the title, another three individual golds and the silver team medal.

Closing the magazine, I remembered the day that I had seen her return from practicing for world competition, and the article rekindled my desire to someday own a Pitts Special.

I jumped on the internet to see what it would take to buy a Pitts, but also to see if I could find some more information on Betty Stewart.

My search kept turning up information and photos on another Betty– Betty Skelton.

Like Betty Stewart, Betty Skelton was a competitive aerobatic pilot, but way before the time that I had seen my first Pitts Special in the skies over Boulder.

Unlike Betty Stewart, Betty Skelton was into setting records on land as well as in the air. She was known as the First Lady of Firsts and had helped create opportunities for women in aviation, auto racing and even advertising. How did I not about *this* Betty, I thought to myself as I read about her life.

~~~

I continued to read about Betty Skelton's accomplishments.

She had set 17 aviation and automobile records in her career. She was a natural when it came to flying, having first flown at the age of 12, the same age as when I had met Betty Stewart.

Betty Skelton got her pilot's license at 16, and even qualified to be a Women Airforce Service Pilot (WASP) but was too young to join. The WASP were discontinued by the time she reached the required age of 18 ½.

Betty was a certified flight instructor by the time she was just 19 years old.

She learned how to fly aerobatics by borrowing a Fairchild PT-19 in 1945, and just a year later she had purchased a Great Lakes sport biplane and entered it into a competition in Jacksonville, Florida. She won, and it was the start of an amazing professional aerobatic career, but also helped her become a test pilot.

She bought a rare Pitts Special in 1948 from the designer of the plane– Curtis Pitts. It was just the second Pitts that had been hand built by Curtis Pitts. It was repainted into a dramatic red and white pattern and was named L'il Stinker.

L'il Stinker would help Betty Skelton become the US Female Aerobatic Champion in 1948, 1949 and 1950. She was famous, but she was frustrated that there were no more challenges in aerobatics, and she couldn't compete with the men. Why? She was a girl.

She retired in 1951 from the air show circuit and sold the Pitts, but went on to set high altitude records in a Piper Cub followed by a world speed record in a P-51 Mustang.

Her friend, Bill France of NASCAR fame, invited her to drive a Pace Car during the 1954 Speed Week at Daytona Beach, Florida. She set a stock car speed record on the beach at Daytona during Speed Week. Flying was her passion, but she discovered a new passion that week.

She would go onto setting four Feminine World Land Speed Records along with a transcontinental speed record. She set a record driving a jet car over 300 miles per hour at Bonneville Salt Flats, then went on to break a record driving the Cannonball Run.

But that wasn't enough for Betty Skelton...

In 1959, Betty was the first woman to undergo NASA's physical and psychological tests, which were identical to those given to the Mercury Seven astronauts. NASA administered the tests at the request of *Look Magazine* for an article. She met and charmed the astronauts with her personality, then impressed them with her pilot skills. They nicknamed her *"7½."* Betty was featured on the February 2, 1960 cover of *Look Magazine*. The title on the cover of the magazine was–

SHOULD A GIRL BE FIRST IN SPACE?

She never got the chance to go to space. No girls ever got the chance go to space in the early days of space flight.

Betty summed up the challenge for women aviators during that time in history by saying, "I complained that NASA wasn't giving more thought to women pilots. I wanted very much to fly in the Navy, but all they would do is laugh when I asked."

The United States Navy eventually awarded Betty her honorary wings. Her response, "Nothing has changed."

~~~

Having read about Betty Skelton, I made a commitment that when I someday got a Pitts that it would be dedicated to Betty, and others who blazed the trail for women's equality in aviation. My search for a Pitts began that day.

~~~

The search started with the original L'il Stinker Pitts that was hanging in the lobby of the Steven F. Udvar-Hazy Center at Washington Dulles International Airport, which is part of the National Air and Space Museum. I called the curator to see if they would sell it, but it was made clear that Betty's original plane would not be an option. Hey I tried…

Next I set out to find a project Pitts to recreate our own L'il Stinker.

Finding a project Pitts did not take long at all, and based on the ease of locating a project plane, I thought that the Pitts would be in the air soon, thrilling crowds as Betty Skelton had once done. I never inspected the plane I ended up purchasing, and relied on photos and written details of the airframe to make a decision to get it delivered, sight unseen. The seller had promised it wouldn't take long to complete the Pitts and get it back in the air. He had just run out of time and money and needed to get rid of it. "It's almost done," was his claim.

However, once the plane was delivered it was clear that it was going to take time and money, lots of it, to get the Pitts anywhere close to flying. It didn't look anything like a plane when the fuselage and wings showed up on my doorstep. The wings had many broken wooden ribs and other pieces were missing. I knew, because the fabric on the wings had been removed. The fuselage was simply a welded steel frame, stripped of paint and missing many major components, like the engine and propeller.

It was disappointing, but I wasn't going to let a little thing like a missing engine or prop get in the way of recreating L'il Stinker III. I immediately contacted several friends who were experts in rebuilding Pitts' type of aircraft to begin the rebuild.

~~~

My friends helped me start the rebuild of the Pitts, saying I could do most of the work, versus spending up to $100 an hour at a shop. The Pitts Special was way harder than any Guillow's balsa wood model that I had built as a kid.

I had no idea how hard the wood and fabric work would be, which is probably what the guy I bought the plane from thought before making the decision to sell. It was a tough, time consuming process to rebuild the Pitts, but I was committed to finishing the biplane in order to fly it to shows and educate folks on the life and accomplishments of Betty Skelton.

~~~

Two years and twenty thousand dollars went by, and the Pitts looked much the same as when it was delivered, only the wings were now repaired and the steel fuselage was repainted. The restoration process had been a huge disappointment up until this point, and the only good news was that the major components were finally ready to be covered in fabric. I couldn't see any end of the money and time being spent on the rebuild and I was ready to give up and put the plane up for sale.

My dream of owning a Pitts and telling the Betty Skelton story was fading.

~~~

An e-mail from the president of the local International Aerobatic Chapter showed up on my computer the day I was going to list the Pitts for sale.

"Hey Gordon. Did you see the request for an uncovered Pitts? You might want to hold off on covering your project," said the e-mail. "A link with the following information is attached."

I opened the link which said that the 70th Anniversary of the first flight of Curtis Pitts' revolutionary biplane was to be featured at the annual EAA AirVenture event in Oshkosh, Wisconsin in 2015. The largest gathering of Pitts Special aircraft were to be on hand at the fly-in, and a request is being sent out to all owners of Pitts Special aircraft looking for an example of an uncovered version of the plane to be on hand for the event. It would be a centerpiece that could be seen by over 500,000 visitors.

I would never in my lifetime have the chance to tell half a million people the Betty Skelton story by flying the Pitts to local airshows, so I held off on listing the plane for sale and contacted the EAA. The delay and disappointment of the restoration could pay off in a way I never imagined.

~~~

Sadly, an uncovered example of a Pitts was available for the EAA AirVenture display that was located just an hour away. I did not get the opportunity to show off my version of L'il Stinker to thousands of interested people and tell Betty's story the way I had hoped.

But the idea of displaying the uncovered Pitts stuck with me. With help, I assembled the plane without fabric and displayed it at the Spirit of Flight museum with information on Betty Skelton and her accomplishments. The display challenges visitors to imagine what the plane will look like when it is fully restored and flying, something that will hopefully happen someday, just as I had imagined as a kid at an airport in Boulder, Colorado.

Encouragement from three women, my grandma, a lady flying a Pitts in Boulder, and the First Lady of Firsts helped me to chase a dream to own a Pitts Special. They all had the same first name, one that I have always liked.

"Who's *your* Betty?"

Chapter Fourteen

The Spirit of Flight

"Is it okay if my son takes a look around while we talk business," asked the guy sitting across from me. We had met to talk about my helping him find a Cessna 182 for family trips.

We were sitting in my office, which had an adjoining warehouse that displayed my hobby out of control, over 1000 aviation artifacts that included a wreck of a Messerschmitt Bf109.

"No problem to look around," I told the dad, as his son's eyes gazed around the office in sensory overload. "Just be careful and please don't touch."

"I'll be careful. Thanks!" said the boy.

I began to pitch a few Cessna 182 aircraft that were available for sale when I was interrupted by the boy.

"Hey, you have WIFI in here?" asked a teenage boy.

"Yeah, why do you ask?" I replied.

"It says, right over there," said the boy as he pointed toward a large bent propeller in the lobby of the office.

"Really? Show me," I said as I got out of my chair. "I know that it's 2004 and early for an office to have WIFI, but no way does it say we have WIFI on anything," I said as I approached the bent prop.

The boy pointed to a small plaque on the propeller.

"See, it says it right there."

I read the plaque, which read- PROPELLER FROM A WWII MESSERSCHMITT BF-109.

"That says WWII, you know, World War Two," I said to the kid in a slightly frustrated tone.

"Oh yeah, I think they talked about that once in school," said the kid as he walked away without any other interest in what he had just looked at. "Can I get online to play a game," the kid asked his father. "Not now son, wait 'til we get home."

~~~

I could not stop thinking about the lack of knowledge that the teenage boy had about World War II as I presented details of the Cessna planes to the dad.

"How could this be?" I asked myself, over and over in frustration.

I asked the dad, "Don't they teach kids about the war in school anymore?"

"Not really. Maybe a day or two a year," he replied. "We really need a place like this for kids to learn about WWII history."

An idea came to me with that comment, an idea that would spiral out of control.

~~~

I began a search for a site to establish a new museum, something different than a standard museum. I wanted to create a gathering place for people who were interested, or maybe not, in aviation and aviation history and I had to have an appropriate name. I thought about what makes people look up to see what is flying overhead. Was it a disease?

Something in the water? Maybe it was an internal bug, or some kind of spirit. As I thought, the name came to me–

The Spirit of Flight Center.

Locations for a new museum included Jeffco Airport in Broomfield, Colorado; Fort Collins/Loveland Airport; Platte Valley Airport in Hudson, Colorado; Front Range Airport in Watkins, Colorado, and Erie Municipal airport where I had learned to fly.

Mesa Arizona was briefly considered, until my wife told me to enjoy my new apartment in Arizona should I put the museum there.

A year went by as we designed a new building, negotiated locations to build it on, and gathered support from friends and family to make the museum a reality. It seemed that everyone had an opinion on where the museum should be and what it should look like. A common statement was, "You know what you ought to do?" followed by "Let me know when the opening is."

Negotiations fell apart on every single location, and always as we were ready to sign a contract. It was a frustrating process that made me wonder if a museum was meant to be a part of my life. I was ready to give up, until one day when a World War II veteran dropped into the warehouse where I had my office.

"Hey Gordy," said the 82 year old as he walked into the office.

It was George Meshko, who was a gunner and flight engineer on a Boeing B-17 during the war.

"I think I found a place for that museum I heard about," said George, as he made his way from the front door to my desk. I fully expected another opinion of what we should do and not much else.

"You know that big green hangar at Erie Municipal?" he asked.

"I think so. Is it the one by your hangar?" I replied.

"That's the one. It's been for sale for five years, and I think you should get it," said George.

I thought to myself, "Great, another opinion of what we should do."

"What's wrong with it that it has been on the market so long?" I asked.

"The owner has turned down 26 offers to date. Looking for the right kind of operation to be in the hangar he built, which was supposed to be some sort of Red Cross training center that didn't work out," said George.

George had actually come up with a good idea for the museum location, and it was already built.

"That could really speed things up for us George," I said.

"Only problem for you will be convincing the owner, who doesn't need to sell, that you are worthy," George replied. "Lots of offers have been turned down."

George handed me a handwritten note that had a name and phone number written on it.

"Give this guy a call," he said. "I hope things can work out."

~~~

I called the number on the note the George had given me and a female realtor answered. After a long conversation of what we intended to do with the building, the realtor said that our offer just might be something the owner of the building would be interested in. She promised to get back to me by the end of the day with an answer. I hung up the phone thinking the new museum had found a home.

At 5:30PM I got a call as promised from the realtor.

"Hey, he will accept your offer and likes your idea of a museum too," she said.

I was thrilled at the news.

"One catch. You have to close on the deal in 30 days or less or the deal is off," she added.

"Thirty days?!" I responded.

"Yeah, I know, but that's his terms. You're not the first to submit an offer," said the realtor.

"Well, let's try to get it done. I'll do my best," I said.

"I'll send over the contract tomorrow. I won't hold my breath on this one," she added as she hung up.

We had a deal, but the stars would have to line up perfectly to get it done.

~~~

Miraculously, things fell into place the next 30 day and we were able to close on a new home for the museum. The Spirit of Flight Center was a reality, but much would need to be done to the facility to turn the museum into what was envisioned. We had a building, we had artifacts, we had financial supporters, and we had the desire and passion to create a world class facility.

What we didn't have was a crystal ball to see what was up ahead. It was November, 2008 and something was about to happen that would change the world.

~ ~ ~

The next sixty days were spent doing major repairs to the building that did not show up in the inspection report. Severe water leaks came from the metal roof of the building and water had damaged the drywall and wood floors. Every wall in the building needed to be cleaned and painted because it had sat in disarray so long.

The building was infested with mice that had made nests in between the walls, and mouse turds were in every drawer and crevasse. The 8' rock wall that surrounded the garden area had fallen over, and a pond in the same area had not been cleaned out for years and smelled like gasoline. The wood fences around the property had blown over in the wind because of wood rot at the bases of the posts. There was major work that needed to be done to ever see the Spirit of Flight open, and there was major money that was needed to be spent on the repairs.

We had a problem as we had spent all the money we had to buy the building and had no reserves for repairs. The other problem was that all of the people who had offered financial support before we had moved into the new building had pulled out. We were in the great recession of 2008 and the future did not look the way we had planned.

~~~

Thanks to dozens of volunteers, including local Girl Scouts, we are able to make repairs, paint and clean, fix fences and rock walls, and countless other tasks to get the museum open to the general public on January 1, 2009. It was an overwhelming effort, but we finally had a home.

Within months, we had donations of artifacts, and even some aircraft to the museum. One of those aircraft was an incredibly rare Cessna L-19 Bird Dog. It was an airplane that I had tried to buy over the last five years, but I was told that the only way it would ever leave the spot where it sat rotting away, was if it were to go to a museum. Now that we had a museum facility, I made another effort to get the plane.

For years, the Cessna L-19 sat in front of what is now Redstone College in Broomfield, Colorado. I had begged the Dean of the College to sell it, but they knew like I did that it was the first Cessna L-19 of the 3,431 aircraft that were built, and they were not interested in letting it go.

I had big plans in my head for the Bird Dog should we have success in prying it away from the college.

Not only was the L-19 a neat looking plane, but it had a cool name which it had received as a result of a contest held with Cessna employees to name the plane. I had thought many times about what a flyable plane could do for a museum in a good or bad economy. Rides could help the museum to generate revenue. The Bird Dog could do the job. But despite my pitch to the college about the museum being a good home, they still did not want to let it go.

The L-19 that sat in front of Redstone College was the prototype aircraft which Cessna used in development of the plane. Because it was the working prototype, it never flew, until a 100 MPH wind storm tore it from the ground tie-downs and sent it on it's one and only flight. It went over the top of a hangar, down a ravine, hit a pine tree and concrete block retaining wall before it came to rest. The wings were curved up on each end, and the fuselage had bent near the tail when it was all over.

I got a call the next day from the dean. "You ready for the Bird Dog?"

"We will be there in an hour," I replied.

We had a Bird Dog! The museum had a centerpiece that could generate revenue.

~~~

The L-19 showed up to the Spirit of Flight Museum the next day, but it was obvious it would take a lot of work to get it back into the air.

Work began, and it would take nearly two years of painstaking restoration and hours of the dirty task of polishing to bring the historic Bird Dog back to life. We were close to getting the plane to flyable condition when we got a call from Cessna Aircraft's legal department.

"Hey Mr. Page. Congratulations on getting the prototype L-19 Bird Dog. Quite a catch," said the lawyer.

"Yeah, we are really excited and almost done with the restoration," I replied.

"Well, we are going to ask you not to fly it," the lawyer said.

"What? We want to do rides at the museum to make some revenue in this bad economy," I said.

"We don't know what kind of metal or processes went into the production, so for liability reasons, we don't want you to fly it," he said.

"Okay, we can honor that request. We would like Cessna to be a sponsor of our non-profit air museum," I told the lawyer.

"Sorry, just laid off 5,000 workers. Your timing is bad," he replied. "Don't fly it," he said as he hung up the phone.

"Well, so much for a ride airplane," I said under my breath. "So much for the revenue."

I was devastated, but there was no way I was going to take on Cessna, just to do rides.

The next week, volunteers from Redstone College and I, hung the Bird Dog from the ceiling of the museum. It took a solid eight hours to hang it and was a job I never wanted to do again in my life.

As we finalized the hanging of the Bird Dog, George Meshko walked into the museum.

"Nice Disco Ball, Gordy," he said. "Is it going to be easy to take down to fly it?"

"Never coming down, George," I said. "Never coming down..."

~~~

Over the next four years, the Spirit of Flight Museum would have over 50,000 visitors from around the world tour the collection to great acclaim. The museum had become a gathering point as I had hoped, and it was rented out for weddings, receptions, fundraisers, and even a swing dance. Thousands of teenagers learned about aviation history, included World War II, which was the main purpose of starting the museum.

The museum became a full-time, non-paying job that brought on many challenges, including the occasional rental that wanted us to take down the Bird Dog because it was in the way of decorations.

The Bird Dog is one of the many planes and other items that permanently hang from the ceiling of the ever growing Spirit of Flight museum.

Starting a museum was one of the hardest things I had ever done, but we overcame obstacles to make it happen.

Funding is still a challenge.

The museum has WIFI.

Chapter Fifteen

Touch and Go

"Annnnd CUT!" said Veronica, a TV producer we had been working with at the Spirit of Flight museum for a potential reality series. "That's a wrap. Nice job!" she added just as my cell phone rang. "Good thing that thing didn't ring when we were filming," said Veronica.

"Sorry, won't happen again," I said as I hit the answer button.

"Hey, it's Geoff," said the guy on the other end of the call.

"You busy?" he asked.

"Just finished filming for a possible TV show, man," "You almost got on the air, since I forgot to turn off my phone," I replied.

"You are always up to something," Geoff said. "Sorry, but I wanted to ask you something. "Can you do an appraisal on a Gulfstream G-II?" he asked.

"Sure. What is it?" I answered as the production assistant came over and unclipped a small microphone off my collar and pulled it down the front of my shirt.

"We got a G-II that we are using to test a new engine in San Antonio, and the boss needs to know what it's worth," Geoff said.

"I can help," I replied, as the production assistant unclipped a microphone transmitter from my belt and spooled the mic wire around it.

"They need you here in three days," said Geoff.

I thought to myself, why am I not surprised?

"Send me the details and I'll be there, Bud."

This was typical of the deals I had in the past with the company Geoff worked for.

~~~

I had met Geoff right after he was hired by a French based company that had US headquarters in Grand Prairie, Texas. I worked with his company indirectly while I was doing simulator software sales and had created some great relationships with people in the company, including Geoff. Eventually, I worked directly for the French company under a contract and was always under the gun to turn things around quickly.

Geoff and I had traveled the world together trying to sell a software product to airlines and corporate flight departments. It was not an easy task to get flight departments to pay to have their flight data monitored by our software. Many thought our software was like "Big Brother" spying on them, but in reality it helped flight departments operate more safely and efficiently.

The bean counters liked the idea of the software helping them save fuel and expense on maintenance and repairs. But the software was new to the industry, which meant that Geoff and I had to work a lot of conventions and visit jet operators constantly to convince them to buy our product. We spent a lot of time together until the day that he took a job in the company to market a new jet engine. The day Geoff left for his new position is the day my contract was cancelled, but Geoff and I promised to stay in contact and work together whenever possible.

"I'll send you the contact," said Geoff. "There might be something else coming up," he added. "Stay tuned."

~~~

I traveled to San Antonio, Texas on a hot July day and arrived at the address my GPS sent me. It was Kelly Air Force Base, which had recently opened up an area of the airport to commercial ventures.

There was a hangar where the GPS said there was, but no driveway to get to it. I could see the nose of a white Gulfstream jet through a garage door, but it wasn't clear how to get to the building, so I drove through the grass and parked in front of the hangar.

As I got out of the car I was immediately yelled at by a guy wearing a yellow vest, and speaking in a thick French accent to move my vehicle. "No parking. This is secure!" he said as he pointed me to a parking lot to the south of the grass field I had just driven through.

After parking my car, I walked back to the garage door and was greeted by a security guard, who unlike the first guy, was not French.

"I'm here to do an appraisal on the jet," I told the guard.

"They said you were going to be here. Sign in, and get a vest," he said as he pointed to a small folding table inside the garage door.

"The boss will be right with you," said the guard as he handed me a well-used, yellow vest.

As I put on the vest, a well-dressed, and well-tanned gentleman walked up to me and introduced himself.

"I'm Luc, thank you for getting here so quickly," he said.

"We are trying to fly the new engine and need insurance, which is why you are here," he added. "We need to know what it is worth."

"No problem," I said. "Just need to inspect the plane and look at the logs." "Won't take long."

"I hope not," said Luc. "We are WAY behind schedule, and I am wanting to retire." "Can't until this plane flies."

"I do my thing and get out of your hair," I said.

"Okay, but please stay out of the way of the engineers, and do NOT pass the red line on the ramp," said Luc. "You might get shot," he added.

"Oh yeah, it's still an active base," I said, as I pulled out my camera from my pocket and opened up a file containing a check list for the inspection.

"Please let me know if you need anything," said Luc, who turned to walk away.

"Remember, we need your report soon," he said as he walked out of the hangar.

~~~

For the next hour I dodged workers and ground equipment as I walked around the Gulfstream G-II taking notes and photos. Overall, the inspection went smoothly. The jet was typical of many Gulfstream jets I had inspected in the past. However, there was a glaring feature on the former executive jet that was different from any I had ever seen. It was the engines. One engine was the original Rolls Royce SPEY, and the other was twice the size, and enclosed in a light blue engine nacelle. It was HUGE, and it was the new engine that my friend Geoff was marketing.

~~~

Two weeks later, I had finished the appraisal of the G-II and provided the report to Luc as promised. He was very happy, but still behind schedule, and still not retired.

~~~

Two months later I got another call from my friend, Geoff.

"Hey, it's Geoff. Remember when I said that something else might be coming up?"

"Yeah. What's up," I answered.

"Do you think you could help out with filming the flight test of the G-II you appraised?" he said. "You are doing a show, right?"

"Yeah. I could ask the producers and see if they are interested, but only if I get to be a part of it," I said.

"There's one catch," Geoff said.

"They need the film for a display at our booth at the NBAA Conference in October. We need to film the flight test next week," he said.

"Well, I will call and get back to you soon," I said. "Hope your budget is big," I added.

"If they get it right, there will be more business," replied Geoff.

I hung up with Geoff and immediately contacted Veronica.

~~~

Timing could not have been better for the production team, and they worked out a deal with Geoff to schedule filming of the flight test in San Antonio. Geoff arranged to be on site for the filming, and I was asked to be at the filming as a technical advisor. A travel schedule was set with the production team, but at the last minute, Veronica got contracted to direct another show.

She put Chris de la Garza, and his filming buddy, Dirk Ruge in charge of arranging and directing the shoot. They had both filmed at the museum and were highly qualified to make the flight test filming a success.

However, in addition to the tight schedule to turn around the film for the conference, there were several other risks factors that stood in the way of success.

Risk factor number one was that Chris planned to drive from Denver to San Antonio pulling a motorcycle trailer he borrowed to carry all of the gear needed for the filming. Because of other projects he was working on, he would have just one day to drive down the gear. If anything happened, such as an accident, break down, inclement weather or theft, the filming was off.

The second risk factor, and maybe the biggest one, was that we only had two days on site to get all of the filming completed, before Chris and the rest of the team had to leave for other film jobs. Should anything delay the flight testing, the trip to do the filming would be a total loss.

The third risk factor was that the filming would occur on an active military base where there was security on every corner. We needed to have prior permission to film, and we did not have written permission in hand when it was time to book our flights.

Finally, Geoff, and the boss he reported to in France, wanted to see a 30 second teaser of what the final product would look like, and they wanted the teaser the night of the first day of filming. If the teaser was bad, they could cancel the rest of the filming and send everyone home.

Chris was undaunted by all that could go wrong, including the editing of a 30 second spot for Geoff. He arranged a team that included two editors and a film shooter from Colorado, then added two additional shooters from Texas. That meant a total of five on the team who would be holding cameras to film the flight testing and all that built up to the first flight of the new jet engine.

The biggest risk of all was that the engine could potentially fail, adding to the stress of things that could go wrong. Despite all that could spell disaster, Chris took a loaded down trailer and a six pack of Red Bull on the non-stop drive to San Antonio, Texas. He was scheduled to arrive one day before the rest of the team who were traveling by air.

~~~

I received an e-mail the night before I was supposed to fly to San Antonio with my flight details. Included in the e-mail was a list of contact names and numbers for everyone who would be on site for the filming. I didn't know any of the names other than Chris and Dirk, and I was a bit nervous by the time I arrived at Denver International the next morning. My name was on the line having referred Chris and his team for the filming, and unlike Chris, I began to focus on things that could go wrong.

Waiting at the gate for the flight to San Antonio, I noticed a lady who was guarding a bright yellow, plastic case that looked like it could be camera gear. I took a chance and asked the lady if she was part of the filming in San Antonio. She laughed. "Yeah, I'm going down there, but things are a bit unorganized," she said.

"I'm Gordon," I replied.

"I saw you name on the list. I'm Meryem," "And this is Scarlet," she said, while patting the bright yellow case.

"This thing is one of the cameras we'll be using on the shoot," she added.

"And here comes Red," she said, as hugged a tall, lanky guy wearing a tee shirt and cargo shorts. He was carrying another yellow case.

"This is Adam," said Meryem.

"Adam and I have worked together on a lot of projects, and we are going to edit on site to meet some deadline," she said.

"Yeah, can't wait," said Adam.

Just then another guy joined our group.

"You guys are on this project," he said.

"Yeah, gonna do another one," said Meryem. "Gordon, this is Jeremiah," she added.

"You got the good cameras," Jerimiah said to Meryem.

She pulled the yellow box tight against her chest, while motioning to Adam to do the same. Adam gave a sinister smile, then faked like he was about the drop his case.

"Not letting these out of my site," Meryem said. "We checked more," she added.

"Man, I hope the shoot is more organized than what has happened so far," Jerimiah said to me just as the gate agent announced that the plane was boarding.

"I have been down there, so hopefully it will go smooth," I said to everyone as we made our way to the gate.

"I really hope," I added under my breath.

~~~

An hour and a half later our plane touched down in San Antonio.

Despite the brief meeting at Denver International, the team quickly joined up like old friends and we made our way to the baggage retrieval.

Meryem was right, there was a ton of other luggage that held the needed items to produce a show.

"We have a van waiting for us," said Meryem, as six big plastic luggage cases were organized and pulled to a waiting van outside the exit doors. "Hope it's a big one," she added.

~~~

Sigrid was a 4th grade teacher in Denver. She was also Dirk's wife, and had taken time off from her job to join the film crew in Texas. She pulled up to the curb of passenger pickup in a Dodge Caravan just as we walked through the exit doors.

"Welcome to Texas," Sigrid said through an open window on the passenger side of the van. "I hope this thing is big enough for all the gear you have," she added.

"Chris made it. He and Dirk are at the hotel waiting for you guys," she said. "Mark and Rico are there too."

I opened the rear cargo door to the van and began to stack the cases and bags. It was clear that some of them would have to go up front with passengers.

"They say that the location looks pretty good," Sigrid said as bags were tossed in between seats and on top of passengers.

"Careful of Red and Scarlet," Meryem said as I picked up one of the yellow cases to put it in the van.

"Got it," I said as the last bag was squeezed into the van. I jumped into an open seat and slid the side door of the van shut. Sigrid eased away from the curb.

"We're about 20 minutes away from the hotel," Sigrid said, as we left the airport and exited onto the highway. "Anyone excited?" she added.

There was no response from anyone other than me. "I'm ready!"

Adam snickered at my comment as he knew what was about to happen.

I was the rookie on this project.

~~~

We arrived at a Holiday Inn Express on the West side of San Antonio in the 20 minutes that Sigrid had predicted. A silver Toyota pickup towing a 10', white motorcycle trailer was parked in front of the entrance of the hotel. It was Chris' truck, which had dodged the first risk factor of the project—it had made it to San Antonio.

We pulled in behind Chris' truck and the team poured out of the van. Bags and cases were unloaded, with Meryem personally handling the yellow cases that help the cameras.

Chris and Dirk were waiting in the lobby of the hotel to greet the team. Chris was full of energy, despite the fourteen hour drive he had made from Colorado.

"Hey guys, meeting in thirty minutes to go over the shoot," Chris said, as the team members were handed room keys by the front desk receptionist.

"Sigrid got you all checked in," Chris said. "Dirk is going to store cameras in his room."

"I'll hang on to mine," said Meryem.

"Drop your stuff and meet me in the conference room in thirty," said Chris. "Thanks for being here guys," he added.

~~~

Half an hour later the team was gathered around a conference table in the hotel meeting room. Chris handed each member a printed schedule, and a copy of a hand drawn storyboard of how he envisioned each scene that was needed to be filmed in order to create the three minute video.

"Remember, we need to do a thirty second teaser," Chris said as he looked at Adam and Meryem.

"Got it," Meryem said, as team members shuffled through the storyboards.

The "shooters" began talking to each other in a language that was foreign to me.

"We should use a slider here, Jibs there, C-Stands over there," were some of the terms. It sounded a bit like the teacher's voice on an episode of Charlie Brown to me. "Wah, wah, wah." I just sat and listened.

I was indeed the rookie on this project and had a lot to learn, mostly to know when I would be in the way of the production. The schedule was tight and the last thing I wanted was to be the guy that got in the way of an already risky schedule.

The meeting lasted an hour before Chris called for adjournment.

"I'm fried and need some sleep," he said. "Sorry, but to stay on schedule, you guys need to be ready to go at 5:30AM."

We were on Central time zone in San Antonio, which meant a 5AM wake-up call, or 4AM, Denver time. Who was I to challenge the early call? Chris was in charge.

~~~

The 5AM wake-up call came fast the next morning. I got ready and headed to the lobby at 5:30AM fully expecting to be the only one ready to go. I was wrong. Dirk had already loaded the gear that was in his room, and the rest of the team was sitting in the lobby with coffee in hand, ready to leave for the shoot. The only one missing from the team was Chris.

Chris showed up at 5:35AM, and like a football team leaving a huddle the team got up and headed to the door.

"Sigrid, follow me," said Chris. "It's about 15 minutes from here," he added. "Starbucks, anyone?" Chris said. "We got time."

Everyone's hands went up in unison to approve the idea.

"I haven't seen any around here, but I'll ask Siri on my phone. She'll find one," said Chris. "Here, take a radio. He handed a small walkie-talkie to me. "Easier than trying to get you on the phone."

I switched it on and pressed the talk button to make sure it worked.

The team members jumped into the van that was packed full of bags of gear. It was a tight fit for everyone. Fortunately we would not have to be in the van too long.

We left the hotel and followed Chris' truck and trailer out of the parking lot and we were soon on an empty highway heading south. Traffic picked up as we got off just one exit down. There was no Starbucks in sight as we continued to follow Chris. Traffic kept building at the early hour.

Chris turned into the entrance of Lackland Air Force base and we were suddenly stuck in line of other cars that were being screened at the security shack of the base. Chris pulled up to a security guard, who motioned for him to drive to a turn around.

"Sorry guys," Chris said over the radio. "There's a Starbucks on the base, but we can't go in. Stupid Siri," he added. "We'll send Sigrid out later."

We followed Chris out of the base and back onto the dark, empty highway.

Fifteen minutes later, we were pulling in front of the hangar at Kelly Air Force Base where I had done the inspection on the G-II just a few weeks before. The garage door to the hangar was open as it was when I had visited, and the plane sat in the same location as before.

As the team members unloaded, we were greeted by the same security guard I had met on my inspection trip.

"You can't park there," he said. "Oh, it's you again," he added as he noticed me.

"We're here to film today," Chris said, just as my friend Geoff emerged from the corner of the open hangar door.

"Hey Bud," Geoff said as he reached out to shake my hand.

"Ready to do this?" he asked. "And by the way, I have an e-mail with permission from the base to film, so don't let me forget to send you that," he added.

"Hey Geoff, I'm Chris. We're ready."

"Well, there are a few things going on that could be a factor," Geoff said.

"We have to stay out of the way of the engineers, because they didn't get in the high speed taxi yesterday as part of the engine test," he said. "They have to do that or they can't fly."

"We only have the two days with this film team," Chris replied.

"Yeah, that's the other problem," said Geoff. "If they don't get the taxi test in today, you might as well go home. It would be a disaster if you don't get what you need for our big show in Florida next month."

"Hey, we know what we have to do, Geoff," said Chris. "We're ready."

"Then let's get going. I need to show you where you can and can't go," said Geoff.

~~~

While Chris and I were talking with Geoff, the rest of the team went into high gear and had unloaded the trailer, along with the cases in the van. Within minutes the area in front of the hangar looked like a movie production set, including a plastic folding table that would be the gathering point for the team members—the "grazing table" for snacks and drinks.

Chris and I were led by Geoff around the Gulfstream and to the large hangar doors which opened to the ramp on the airport side of the building.

"See that red line?" Geoff asked.

"Yeah, yeah, you get shot if you pass the line," I said.

Chris' eyes opened wide. "You're kidding, right?"

"He's right," answered Geoff.

"Gordon knows his way around the plane and the base, so make sure you ask before doing *anything*," said Geoff.

"I knew there was a reason to have you here," Chris said as he patted me on the shoulder.

Geoff continued to walk us around the hangar, introducing us to some of the engineers, then showing us to a small conference room. "You can put the editors in here so they can download the hard drives from the filming and do their thing," Geoff said, as he opened the door. "Remember the 30 second teaser, Chris."

"This works, and I haven't forgotten, Geoff," replied Chris. "Let's get going."

Chris walked to the grazing table where the film team had gathered for a morning snack. Sigrid had left in the van to get coffee.

"Alright guys, come with me for a quick tour and to learn some rules so you don't get shot," Chris said. Adam snickered as the team followed Chris, who was joined by Dirk. "How's it look?" Dirk asked Chris.

"Gonna be interesting, but we'll get it done." Chris then handed all of the shooters a small two way radio and asked them to test them. "You and Geoff get one too," he said as he handed us radios.

"Follow me, gang," said Chris. "Editors over there." He pointed. "Shooters over there."

Chris took Meryem and Adam to the small conference room and told them to go ahead and get set up for hard drive dumps from the day.

Chris walked to an area near the unfolded entrance stairs of the Gulfstream. Mark, Jerimiah and Rico began asking Chris and Dirk technical questions about the setup, the equipment needed, angles for shooting, filters and lighting. After a quick volley of questions and answers, the shooters left the building and quickly returned with film cameras and pieces of pipe they began to assemble.

Within minutes, what looked like a small railroad section had been assembled in front of the Gulfstream. "Test out the slider with Red," Chris told Mark.

Mark pulled a film camera from one of Meryem's yellow cases. He attached the camera to a base that had skateboard wheels attached to it. He placed the base onto the track and tested the system. "Work's great, Chris," Mark said has he gently pushed the camera back and forth on the track.

Dirk and Jerimiah had assembled a system that looked like a Giraffe's neck which would elevate a camera to a desired position. "We're ready," Dirk yelled at Chris.

"Geoff, were ready to go," Chris said.

"Sorry, the engineers just told me that it will be an hour or two," Geoff said. "They also said that once there is an "all-go," we have about ten minutes from then before the taxi test. They also want everyone to put on yellow vests."

"No problem," Chris replied.

"Hey gang," Chris yelled out. "Start grabbing B-Roll." "Make sure Meryem and Adam get your drives," he added.

Mark, Jerimiah and Dirk started filming. They would do a shot, then redo it from a slightly different angle, then do it again.

"Dirk," yelled Chris. "I need your help putting some GoPros on the plane."

Just then, a team of six engineers walked into the hangar. They picked up a 5' by 10' blue engine nacelle and began to walk it toward a huge wooden platform that surrounded the new engine that was to be tested.

"What's going on Geoff?" yelled Chris. "Thought you said we had an hour or two?"

"They are just going to fit up the engine cover," Geoff said. "It could take a while working up there. They call the platform, "The Gallows.""

"No problem, we are going to grab some B-Roll until we are ready," Chris said.

"I just got yelled at by the lead engineer," Geoff told Chris.

"Not only will you get shot if you go past that red line, but you can't film anything military or even toward the military ramp."

"Great, essentially giving us half the area to film," responded Chris.

"Sorry, just one more thing to deal with," Geoff replied while shrugging his shoulders, just as an F-16 took off in the background.

~~~

Dirk carefully worked around the engineers that were fitting up the engine cowling, filming every crazy angle he could twist to. They engineers did not seem to care, until Dirk set up a ladder to climb up on top of the engine in order to mount a GoPro.

I held the ladder while Dirk climbed up with the camera, telling him where to place his feet to not damage anything.

One of the engineers on the Gallows yelled down to a guy in French. Minutes later, Geoff was getting scolded, and he carried the message to Dirk saying, "They are going to kill you if you get in the way or step on the wrong part of the engine pylon."

"My fault, Geoff. I told Dirk where to step and he's being careful," I said.

"It better be a helluva shot from up there," Geoff replied.

~~~

Two hours later…

The shooters had exhausted all angles to get B-Roll film. One by one, they would take full hard drives of film to the conference room for Meryem and Adam to download.

I spent a half hour cleaning windows and wiping down the leading edge of the jets wing. Even those efforts were caught on film.

"Hey, where's Sigrid?" asked Dirk. "She's been gone for hours, and I know that there's a Starbucks nearby."

Just then, the white van pulled up to the front of the hangar and Sigrid got out.

"Oh my God, a puppy got hit by a car on my way to coffee, and nobody was doing anything about it," she said, visibly shaken.

The film team gathered around her to hear a story about how she had seen a puppy hurt by a hit and run, and how she had spent the last few hours knocking on doors to find the owner.

"Nobody cared," she said. "They said it happens all the time here, but I finally found the owner." "Sorry it took so long," she said as she started handing out coffee to everyone.

Before anyone could take a drink, a group of engineers entered the building and began to put on yellow vests.

It was go time for the taxi test.

~~~

"Places everyone," Chris directed.

The shooters grabbed their cameras and set up in the pre-planned areas for what was about to happen.

"Jerimiah, grab Scarlet and head to the other side of the runway to film from there," said Chris. "Gordon, you take him there with my truck," he added. "Take a ladder. It will be the most important footage, especially if they don't fly."

"You got it," responded Jerimiah, as he grabbed the camera and asked me to take a tall ladder to the truck.

"I know where to go," I said to Jerimiah as we loaded up and were about to drive to the opposite side of the airport.

Chris and the rest of the film crew would get footage of the test pilots coming out to the plane, the start-up and taxi. At the last minute, Chris directed Dirk to go to the end of the runway to film the jet powering up from the rear of the plane.

Dirk grabbed his camera and asked if we could drop him off in his position on our way to the other side of the field.

"Sure, let's go!" I said as Dirk loaded up his gear.

We drove as fast as we could, hoping no military police would stop us for speeding.

We dropped Dirk into position, then Jerimiah and I drove him to his position, which was about 100 yards from the main entrance to Kelly Air Force Base.

We unloaded and set up the ladder. Jerimiah began to set up a base on the top of the ladder when Chris' voice came over the radio. "They have a problem. Engine is not starting," he said. "Could be a few minutes, so just stay in position."

Cars slowed as they drove by our setup. Most were headed to the main entrance of the base.

"Gordon, this is Dirk," came over the radio.

"Go ahead," I responded.

"I forgot an adapter that's in the truck. Can you bring it to me?" he said.

"On my way," I said clicking the talk button on the radio.

"Be right back, Jerimiah," I said as I got into the truck. "Don't get in trouble while I'm gone," I said sarcastically as I started the engine

~~~

Dirk opened the gate on the truck and grabbed a small bag.

'I'm good, get back to your position," he said.

Jerimiah's voice came over the radio. "Uh, military police. Need help."

"I'll be right there," I responded on the radio.

"Hey Geoff?" "Remember that e-mail with permission?" "I need it NOW!" I radioed.

"Just sent it to you," Geoff said as I pulled up to Jerimiah's position. The ladder was down on its side and Jerimiah had his hands up as two military police officers stood near their police car, hands on their holstered guns.

I got out of the truck and walked to the officers.

"Surely, you guys are not THAT stupid to be filming on a military base without permission," said one of the officers.

"We have permission to film that Gulfstream over there," I answered.

"It's on my phone," I said while reaching for my cell phone.

The police officers flinched and opened their hands on their guns.

"Hold on. Take the phone out *slowly*," said the same officer as before as the other stayed on silent guard.

I handed the officer my phone just as it buzzed with a message. "Hopefully it's from Geoff," I said to myself as I clicked to open the message. It was from Geoff.

"Give me your ID, and wait here while I check this out," said the officer.

I assured Jerimiah that there would be no problems. Hopefully.

~~~

After looking at my phone and checking out my ID, the officer walked over and handed my cell and IDs back to me and Jerimiah.

"They said that your permission is for tomorrow, not today. Take it down," the officer said.

"Can I make a call?" I asked the officer. "I think we have a small mix up."

He shrugged his shoulders, not objecting to my request.

I called Geoff and told him about the situation. He said that he would call a number he had just in case of such an emergency.

"Dude, we don't have much time," I said. He assured me that he would get the problem resolved and hung up.

"Officer, we have an approval coming from the Base Commander in a minute. Can you hold on? We *have* to get this filming done."

"No permission, no film. Keep your camera gear on the ground," he answered.

Jerimiah stood quietly.

A long five minutes later, my phone rang. It was Geoff.

"I got it. Let me talk to the officer."

I handed the phone to the officer who spoke briefly with Geoff, ending the call with "I'll call to confirm."

"Keep the gear down until I make this call," said the officer as he dialed numbers on his cell phone, then turned away so we could not see him during the phone call. He turned around to face us after a brief conversation.

"You're okay this time, but make sure you have your docs lined up in the future," said the officer as he and the other officer walked to their car.

They slammed their doors and drove off as Chris' voice came over the radio.

"The pilots just loaded up again. Engines are starting!" Chris said.

Jerimiah tilted the ladder back up into position and began filming just as the Gulfstream taxied away from the hangar.

The jet followed the taxiway to the end of the runway, then lined up for the taxi test. Full power was added and the G-II began to roll. Soon, it was at the speed to rotate into flight, but instead the engines were cut and brakes were applied to slow the jet. It turned near the mid field point and slowly made its way back to the hangar where it had started from.

The entire event lasted less than ten minutes, but the stress from the military police had taken a few years off of my life.

Chris was once again on the radio. "Did you get it, Jerimiah?

"I got what we need," responded Jerimiah as he took the expensive camera down the ladder.

"Let's see!" said Chris

We loaded our gear, drove to pick up Dirk, then headed back to the hangar.

It was time to deliver a hard drive of film that hopefully had the footage needed for the day.

The clock was ticking for a 30 second teaser that needed to be sent to France that night.

~~~

Adam, Meryem and Chris stayed up until 3AM editing over nine hours of film, down to a thirty second spot. The result was amazing, and the French agreed.

We were a "'go" for day two.

~~~

"Grab more B-roll," Chris said to the film crew as they set up for the second day of shooting at the hangar.

"We need to get ready for the test flight also," Chris added.

The film crew hurried about setting up the equipment that had been taken down the night before.

Chris wanted to have cameras in the same position as the day before to capture the test flight, including the camera by the base entrance. In addition, he wanted to have a camera at both ends of the runway to capture the takeoff and landing of the test flight.

Anxiety was high, as this was the last, and only day that filming could occur. Everything would have to fall in place to capture the flight. The wait was on for the engineers to show up, move the "Gallows" away, push the jet out, then hope the new engine performed as expected to get the test flight in.

~~~

Six hours later…

"Sorry Chris, I've got to go to catch my flight," Dirk said. He had another film job in Colorado to get to.

"I know that takes out a shooter, but Rico can film at my position," Dirk added.

"Get out of here," Chris said, as he gave Dirk a hug. "We'll make it work."

~~~

Two hours later…

"We're gonna run out of light," Chris said to Geoff.

"Sorry, Chris." "I don't have any control," Geoff said, just as his cell phone rang.

Geoff took the call, then almost immediately hung up.

"They're on the way!" Geoff said.

"Places everyone," yelled Chris. "Rico, go with Jerimiah to your position. Gordon, come with me."

A flurry of activity began as the entire purpose of the filming project was about to happen.

"Don't get arrested today!" I said to Jerimiah, as he got into the van with Rico. He did not look amused as he slammed the door and drove away.

Chris and I drove to the opposite end of the runway and took a position where you could barely see the other end where the Gulfstream would begin the test flight.

"I'm going to stand on top of my truck topper to get a better view," Chris said. "Hand me my gear," he added.

He climbed up from the lift gate of the pickup and crawled on his hands and knees on the topper. The topper creaked and popped as he slowly took a seat.

Just then, a massive C-5 Galaxy transport jet flew overhead, having just taken off.

Geoff's voice came over the radio. "The pilots are on board and the door is closed."

"Hand me the camera, quick!" said Chris.

"The engines are starting, the engines are starting," Geoff said over the radio.

Chris put his radio to his mouth and clicked the talk button.

"Everyone ready?" he said.

One by one, the shooters confirmed over the radio that cameras were rolling.

"They are taxiing out," said Geoff.

"Here we go," Chris said to me. "Here, we go."

For the first time during the filming, I saw the stress on Chris' face as he looked into the camera.

The Gulfstream began to move toward the end of the runway.

"Guys, I have a problem," said Jerimiah over the radio.

"You have got to be kidding," I said to Chris. "I thought we had security clearance."

"Go ahead, Jerimiah," Chris responded.

"Just kidding, all is good," said Jerimiah.

"You just bought the first round tonight," Chris said over the radio.

The jet took position on the runway and a large plume of black smoke poured out of the Rolls-Royce Spey engine on the left side of the G-II as full power was added.

The Gulfstream gained speed as it moved toward me and Chris, and unlike the day before, it continued down the runway, past the midfield point. The jet rotated and lifted to the sky. The landing gear folded into the plane as it climbed.

"Got it, got it," said Chris as the jet continued toward our position.

The plane passed overhead, like the C-5 had just minutes before, and flew south. Chris continued filming until it was out of site.

"Guys, the engineering team is cheering," Geoff said over the radio.

"We got it, Geoff," responded Chris.

Then one by one, the other shooters checked in that they had gotten the film that they had hoped for.

Darkness was setting in and the option to film a landing of the test faded.

"That's a wrap," Chris radioed the team. "See you guys at the trailer."

"Well, let's hope we got what we need to make a great video," Chris said, as we got into his truck and drove back to the hangar.

We arrived at the hangar, where the film crew was beginning to break down equipment in preparation to wrap up the filming. Geoff was waiting for us at the trailer.

"Well?" he asked Chris as he got out of the truck.

"I think we have it, Geoff," Chris replied.

"I hope so. That teaser video set a high bar with my boss, so I hope the one for NBAA is that good." Geoff said.

"You have sixty days until the show and the clock is ticking. Please don't let me down," Geoff added as he looked my way.

The first part of the filming project was over, and any looming disasters had been averted.

The next part of the project was in the hands of the editors who would need to work day and night to get a final product for the NBAA show.

~~~

Sixty days later...

"You clean up nice," I told Chris, as we watched a video on a large monitor in a booth at the NBAA Conference in Orlando. It was playing the final version of the three minute video that Chris and his team had produced from over fifteen hours of film.

"You did it!" said a voice from behind. It was Geoff.

"It turned out fantastic!" Geoff said, as several men and women speaking in French walked up to the monitor and began to watch the video. Dramatic music played on the video as the G-II took off to the cheers of the engineering team who watched on. The video was a cinematic masterpiece.

"My bosses love it," Geoff added.

"It was a fun project," Chris replied. "Looking forward to doing more with you," he added as he walked over to a large mockup of a jet engine on display.

"So, what's the next project, Geoff?" I asked.

"There just might be something else coming up," Geoff said with a wink. "You'll be the first to know," he added.

"What's *your* next project?" asked Geoff. "You are always up to something."

"That's an understatement," I said with a smile.

"Stay tuned, my friend."

Epilogue

"That will be $5 for admission. Your son is no charge," I said, as I checked in a visitor into the Spirit of Flight museum.

He was holding a young boy in his arms. "I don't know what ever got into him. He's just crazy about planes, and he just turned two!" he said as he pulled a five out of his pocket and handed it to me.

I rang in the admission fee, then handed the father of the young boy a museum magazine and a coloring sheet for his son.

The young boy was gazing around the museum in awe in his dad's arms.

"He came into the world just loving planes," the father said as he gently pulled the brim of a tiny baseball hat on the boys head. The hat was embroidered with the outline of an F-15. The boy continued his gaze as his father lowered him to the floor and reached out for his son's hand.

"There is a ton to look at today, but I will guess that your son will want to stay in the pedal plane," I said as I pointed to the far side of the museum, where a vintage pedal plane sat.

"I think I know why your son is nuts about planes," I told the dad. "I have the same problem."

"Yeah, what's that?" he said.

"It's why we call this place the Spirit of Flight," I replied. "Spirit of Flight means you have an aviation bug you get inside of you that makes you look up at whatever is flying overhead."

"That's him!" said the father of the young boy.

Just then, the boy pointed to a Cessna L-19 Bird Dog hanging from the ceiling.

"*Airplane!*" he yelled.

"Airplane was his first word," said the dad. "He runs to the door at the house whenever he hears a plane."

"Hate to tell you, but there's not much you can do from here," I replied. "He's got the bug."

"Let's go son," said the dad, as he pulled his son's arm in the direction of the pedal plane.

"Enjoy the museum," I said, as I thought about my own, internal spirit of flight.

The spirit of flight had taken me to many far-away places in my life to fuel my passion for anything aviation.

That passion almost got me killed along the way, but it helped me do something I loved to do.

I was chasing planes.

Appendix

The Cessna T-210

The Cessna 210 Centurion is a six-seat, high-performance, retractable-gear, single-engine, high-wing general aviation aircraft which was first flown in January 1957 and produced by Cessna until 1985.

Specifications

- Crew: One
- Capacity: Five passengers
- Length: 28 ft 2 in
- Wingspan: 36 ft 9 in
- Height: 9 ft 8 in
- Wing area: 175 ft²
- Empty weight: 2,303 lb
- Max. takeoff weight: 4,000 lb
- Powerplant: 1 × Continental Motors TSIO-520-R air-cooled turbocharged flat-six, 310 hp

Number built: 9240

Number owned by the author: One

The Avro Vulcan

The Avro Vulcan is a jet-powered delta wing strategic bomber, which was operated by the Royal Air Force from 1956 until 1984. Aircraft manufacturer A.V. Roe and Company designed the Vulcan in response to Specification B.35/46.

Nicknames: *Iron Overcast; The Tin Triangle*

Specifications (B.Mk 2):

- Engines: Four 20,000-pound thrust Rolls-Royce Olympus 301 turbojets
- Max Takeoff Weight: ~250,000 lbs.
- Wing Span: 111ft. 0in.
- Length: 99ft. 11in.
- Height: 27ft. 2in.
- Performance:
- Maximum Speed: 645 mph
- Ceiling: 65,000 ft.
- Range: 4,600 miles with normal bomb-load
- Armament: Up to 21,000 pounds of bombs, carried internally

Number Built: 134

Number Still Airworthy: One

The Douglas Skyraider

The Douglas A-1 Skyraider (formerly AD) was an American single-seat attack aircraft that saw service between the late 1940s and early 1980s. The Skyraider had a remarkably long and successful career; it became a piston-powered, propeller-driven anachronism in the jet age, and was nicknamed "Spad," after the French World War I fighter.

It was operated by the United States Navy (USN), the United States Marine Corps (USMC) and the United States Air Force (USAF), and also saw service with the British Royal Navy, the French Air Force, the Air Force of the Republic of Vietnam (VNAF), and others. In U.S. service it was finally replaced by the LTV A-7 Corsair II swept wing subsonic jet in the early 1970s.

Nicknames: *Able Dog; Sandy; Spad; Hobo; Firefly; Zorro; The Big Gun; Old Faithful; Old Miscellaneous; Fat Face* (AD-5 version)*; Guppy* (AD-5W version)*; Q-Bird* (AD-1Q/AD-5Q versions)*; Flying Dumptruck* (A-1E)*; Crazy Water Buffalo* (South Vietnamese nickname).

Specifications (AD-7 / A-1J):

- Engine: 2800hp Wright R-3350-26B radial piston engine
- Weight: Empty 10,550 lbs., Max Takeoff 25,000 lbs.
- Wing Span: 50ft. 9in.
- Length: 38ft. 10in.

- Height: 15ft. 8.25in.
- Performance:
- Maximum Speed at 18,000ft: 320mph
- Cruising Speed at 6,000ft: 190mph
- Ceiling: 25,500ft
- Range: 900 miles
- Armament: Four 20mm cannon
- 8,000lbs of hardpoint-mounted freefall and/or forward-firing weapons

Number Built: 3,180 **Number Still Airworthy:** Approx. 19

The Mikoyan MiG 29

The Mikoyan MiG-29 (NATO reporting name: "Fulcrum") is a twin-engine jet fighter aircraft designed in the Soviet Union. Developed by the Mikoyan design bureau as an air superiority fighter during the 1970s, the MiG-29, along with the larger Sukhoi Su-27, was developed to counter new American fighters such as the McDonnell Douglas F-15 Eagle, and the General Dynamics F-16 Fighting Falcon. The MiG-29 entered service with the Soviet Air Force in 1983.

General characteristics

- Crew: 1 (Mig 29 UB: 2)
- Length: 17.37 m (57 ft)
- Wingspan: 11.4 m (37 ft 3 in)
- Height: 4.73 m (15 ft 6 in)
- Wing area: 38 m² (409 ft²)
- Empty weight: 11,000 kg (24,250 lb)
- Loaded weight: 15,300 kg (33,730 lb)
- Max. takeoff weight: 20,000 kg (44,100 lb)
- Powerplant: 2 × Klimov RD-33 afterburning turbofans, 8,300 kgf (81.4 kN, 18,300 lbf) each
- Fuel capacity: 3,500 kg. (7,716 lbs.) internal

Performance

- Maximum speed: Mach 2.25 (1,490 mph) At low altitude: Mach 1.25 (930 mph)
- Range: 888 mi with maximum internal fuel
- Ferry range: 1,300 mi with external drop tanks
- Service ceiling: 59,100 ft
- Rate of climb: initial 65,000 ft/min
- Wing loading: 82 lb/ft²
- Thrust/weight: 1.09
- Maximum design g-load: +9 g

Armament

- 1 x 30 mm GSh-30-1 cannon with 150 rounds
- 9 Hard points: 6 x pylons under-wing, 3 x under fuselage
- Up to 3,500 kg (7,720 lb) of weapons including six air-to-air missiles — a mix of semi-active radar homing (SARH)/infrared homing AA-8 "Aphid", AA-10 "Alamo", AA-11 "Archer", active radar homing AA-12 "Adder", FAB 500-M62, FAB-1000, TN-100, ECM Pods, S-24 rockets, Kh-25, Kh-29

Number of flying MiG 29s in civilian hands: Two

The Ilyushin IL-2

The Ilyushin Il-2 Sturmovik was a ground-attack aircraft in the Second World War produced by the Soviet Union in very large numbers. With 36,183 examples of the Il-2 produced during the war, and in combination with its successor, the Ilyushin Il-10, a total of 42,330 were built, making it the single most produced military aircraft design in aviation history, as well as one of the most produced piloted aircraft in history along with the American postwar civilian Cessna 172 and the Soviet Union's own Polikarpov Po-2 *Kukuruznik* biplane, itself sometimes seen side-by-side with the big armored Ilyushin monoplane on the front lines.

General characteristics

- Crew: Two, pilot and rear gunner
- Length: 11.6 m (38 ft 1 in)
- Wingspan: 14.6 m (47 ft 11 in)
- Height: 4.2 m (13 ft 9 in)
- Wing area: 38.5 m² (414 ft²)
- Empty weight: 4,360 kg (9,612 lb)
- Loaded weight: 6,160 kg (13,580 lb)
- Max. takeoff weight: 6,380 kg (14,065 lb)
- Powerplant: 1 × Mikulin AM-38F liquid-cooled V-12, 1,285 kW (1,720 hp)

Performance

- Maximum speed: 414 km/h (257 mph)
- Range: 720 km (450 mi)
- Service ceiling: 5,500 m (18,045 ft)
- Rate of climb: 10.4 m/s (2,050 ft/min)
- Wing loading: 160 kg/m² (31.3 lb/ft²)
- Power/mass: 0.21 kW/kg (0.13 hp/lb)

Armament

- 2 × fixed forward-firing 23 mm caliber VYa-23 cannons, 150 rounds per gun
- 2 × fixed forward-firing 7.62 mm ShKAS machine guns, 750 rounds per gun
- 1 × manually aimed 12.7 mm Berezin UBT machine gun in rear cockpit, 300 rounds
- Up to 600 kg (1,320 lb) of bombs and/ 8 × RS-82 rockets 4 × RS-132 rockets

Number built: 36,183

Number known to exist: 10

Number flying: 1

The Messerschmitt Me262

The Messerschmitt Me 262 *Schwalbe* (English: "Swallow") of Nazi Germany was the world's first operational jet-powered fighter aircraft. Design work started before World War II began, but engine problems and top-level interference kept the aircraft from operational status with the Luftwaffe until mid-1944. Heavily armed, it was faster than any Allied fighter, including the British jet-powered Gloster Meteor. One of the most advanced aviation designs in operational use during World War II, the Me 262 was used in a variety of roles, including light bomber, reconnaissance and even experimental night fighter versions.

Nicknames: *Turbo* (Used by German pilots.)

Specifications (Me 262A-1a):

- Engines: Two 1,984-pound thrust Junkers Jumo 004B-1/-2/-3 turbojets (Modern replicas to be powered by General Electric J85 axial-flow turbojets).
- Weight: Empty 8,378 lbs., Max Takeoff 14,110 lbs.
- Wing Span: 40ft. 11.5in.
- Length: 34ft. 9.5in.
- Height: 12ft. 7in.
- Performance:
- Maximum Speed: 540 mph

- Ceiling: 37,565 ft.
- Range: 652 miles
- Armament: Four 30-mm MK 108 cannon in nose

Number Built: 1,433

Number Still Airworthy: Three replicas

The Boeing B-29

The Boeing B-29 Superfortress is a four-engine propeller-driven heavy bomber designed by Boeing that was flown primarily by the United States toward the end of World War II and during the Korean War. It was one of the largest aircraft to have seen service during World War II and a very advanced bomber for its time, with features such as a pressurized cabin, an electronic fire-control system, and a quartet of remote-controlled machine-gun turrets operated by the fire-control system in addition to its defensive tail gun installation.

The name "Superfortress" was derived from that of its well-known predecessor, the B-17 Flying Fortress. Although designed as a high-altitude strategic bomber, and initially used in this role against the Empire of Japan, these attacks proved to be disappointing; as a result the B-29 became the primary aircraft used in the American firebombing campaign, and was used extensively in low-altitude night-time incendiary bombing missions. One of the B-29's final roles during World War II was carrying out the atomic bomb attacks on Hiroshima and Nagasaki.

Nicknames: *Washington* (RAF name for B-29s loaned to the UK between 1950-1958); *Bull* (NATO code name for Russian TU-4, a near-exact copy of the B-29).

Specifications:

- Engines: Four 2,200-hp Wright R-3350-23-23A/-41 Cyclone 18 turbocharged radial piston engines.
- Weight: Empty 70,140 lbs., Max Takeoff 124,000 lbs.
- Wing Span: 141ft. 3in
- Length: 99ft. 0in.
- Height: 29ft. 7in.
- Performance:
- Maximum Speed: 358 mph
- Cruising Speed: 230 mph
- Ceiling: 31,850 ft.
- Range: 3,250 miles
- Armament: Two 12.7-mm (0.5-inch) machine guns in each of remote-controlled turrets, plus three 12.7-mm (0.5-inch) machine guns, or two 12.7-mm guns and one 20-mm cannon in the tail turret.

Number Built: 3,970

Number Still Airworthy: One

The 1905 Wright Flyer III

The Wright Flyer III was the third powered aircraft by the Wright Brothers, built during the winter of 1904-05. Orville Wright made the first flight with it on June 23, 1905. The Flyer III had an airframe of spruce construction with a wing camber of 1-in-20 as used in 1903, rather than the less effective 1-in-25 used in 1904. The new machine was equipped with the engine and other hardware from the scrapped Flyer II and—after major modifications—achieved much greater performance than Flyers I and II.

General characteristics

- Crew: one pilot
- Length: 28 ft 0 in
- Wingspan: 40 ft 4 in
- Height: 8 ft 0 in
- Wing area: 503 ft²
- Loaded weight: 710 lb
- Max. takeoff weight: 710 lb
- Powerplant: 1 × Wrights' water-cooled, 4-cylinder, inline engine, 20 hp
- Propellers: Wrights' elliptical propellers later changed to Wrights' "bent-end" propellers propeller, 2 per engine

Performance

- Maximum speed: 35 mph
- Range: 25 miles as of October 1905
- Service ceiling: 50 to 100 ft
- Wing loading: 1.4 lb/ft²
- Power/mass: 0.03 hp/lb

The Grumman Albatross

The Grumman HU-16 Albatross is a large twin–radial engine amphibious flying boat that was used by the U.S. Air Force (USAF), the U.S. Navy (USN) and the U.S. Coast Guard (USCG), primarily as a search and rescue and combat search and rescue aircraft. Originally designated as the SA-16 for the USAF and the JR2F-1 and UF-1 for the USN and USCG, it was re-designated as the HU-16 in 1962.

The final official Grumman classification was *G-111*, devised in the 1970s as the result of a collaborative effort between the manufacturer and Resorts International to convert the military aircraft to an airliner. Of the 57 surplus aircraft purchased for rehabbing, 12 were completed and placed in storage by Chalk Airlines of Miami, where they remain.

General characteristics

- Crew: 4-6
- Capacity: 10 passengers
- Length: 62 ft 10 in
- Wingspan: 96 ft 8 in
- Height: 25 ft 10 in
- Wing area: 1035 ft²
- Empty weight: 22,883 lb
- Loaded weight: 30,353 lb
- Max. takeoff weight: 37,500 lb

- Powerplant: 2 × Wright R-1820-76 Cyclone 9 nine-cylinder single-row air-cooled radial engine, 1,425 hp each
- Fuel Capacity: 675 US Gallons internally, plus 400 US Gal in wingtip floats plus two 300 US Gallon drop tanks

Performance

- Maximum speed: 236 mph
- Cruise speed:124 mph
- Stall speed: 74 mph
- Range: 2,850 mi
- Service ceiling: 21,500 ft
- Rate of climb: 1,450 ft/min

Armament: None **Number Built:** 464, plus 2 prototypes

The Pitts Special

Curtis Pitts began the design of a single-seat aerobatic biplane in 1943–1944. The design has been refined continuously since the prototype's first flight in September 1944, however, the current Pitts S2 still remains quite close to the original in concept and in design.

Several of the aircraft that Curtis Pitts built had a picture of a skunk on them and were called "Stinkers." After she bought it, aerobatic performer Betty Skelton called the second aircraft that Curtis built, "Lil' Stinker." The prototype S-2, which was the first two-seat Pitts, was "Big Stinker," the prototype Model 11 (later called S1-11B) was "Super Stinker," and the prototype Model 12 was the "Macho Stinker."

General characteristics- Pitts S1-C

- Seats: One
- Length: 15.46 ft.
- Wingspan: 17.33 ft.
- Height: 6.29 ft.
- Wing area: 98.47 ft²
- Empty weight: 720 lb
- Max. takeoff weight: 1,150 lb.
- Powerplant: 1 × Textron Lycoming AEIO-360 flat-four air cooled piston engine, 180 hp

Performance

- Never exceed speed: 203 mph
- Cruise speed: 154 mph
- Stall speed: 57 mph
- Range: 240 miles
- Service ceiling: 21,000 ft
- Rate of climb: 1.750 ft/min
- Wing loading: 11.68 lb/ft^2

The Gulfstream G-II

The Gulfstream II (G-II) is an American twin engine business jet designed and built by Grumman and then in succession, Grumman American and finally Gulfstream American. Its Grumman model number is G-1159, and its US military designation is C-11 Gulfstream II. It has been succeeded by the Gulfstream III. The first Gulfstream II flew on October 2, 1966.

Of note, a modified version of the G-II, called the Shuttle Training Aircraft (STA), mimicked the cockpit configuration and flight characteristics of the Space Shuttle, and was used by NASA as a training airplane for practice shuttle approaches (referred to as "dives"). Four G-IIs were used for this purpose.

General characteristics

- Crew: 2
- Capacity: 19 (maximum certified)
- Length: 79 ft 11 in
- Wingspan: 68 ft 10 in
- Height: 24 ft 6 in
- Wing area: 809.6 ft²
- Empty weight: 36,544 lb
- Gross weight: 65,500 lb
- Powerplant: 2 × Rolls-Royce Spey 511-8 turbofan, 11,400 lbf

Performance

- Maximum speed: 581 mph
- Maximum speed: Mach 0.85
- Cruise speed: 483 mph
- Range: 4,123 miles
- Service ceiling: 45,000 ft

Glossary of Aviation Terms

AGL	Above Ground Level
AOA	Angle of Attack
AOG	Aircraft on Ground
ADF	Automatic Direction Finder
ASI	Air Speed Indicator
ATC	Air Traffic Control
CFR	Code of Federal Regulations
COA	Certificate of Authorization
DME	Distance Measuring Equipment
EGT	Exhaust Gas Temperature
FAA	Federal Aviation Administration
FAR	Federal Aviation Regulation
FBO	Fixed Base Operator
FDM	Flight Data Monitoring
GA	General Aviation
GPS	Global Positioning System
IAP	Initial Approach Procedure
ILS	Instrument Landing System
IFR	Instrument Flight Rules
KIAS	Knots Indicated Airspeed
NOTAM	Notice to Airman
PIC	Pilot In Command
SIC	Second In Command
SOP	Standard Operating Procedures
SMOH	Since Major Overhaul (Engine)

TAS	True Airspeed
TFR	Temporary Flight Restriction
TTAF	Total Time Airframe
VFR	Visual Flight Rules

Acknowledgements

Thank you to the following:

Spirit of Flight Center, Erie, Colorado, www.spiritofflight.com
Air Assets International, www.airassets.com
Robert Collings, www.collingsfoundation.org
Buck Wyndham, www.warbirdalley.com
Legend Flyers & Bob Hammer, www.stormbirds.com
www.eaa.org
www.commemorativeairforce.org
www.vulcantothesky.org
www.iac.org
www.aviataircraft.com
www.gulfstream.com

Jane's All the World's Aircraft 1988–89
Jane's Aircraft Upgrades 2008-2009
Sharpe, 2000
Kerplode Productions

To Jim Mills, Tracey Page, Maggie Rowe, Chuck Davis, Kim Peticolas, Becky Hutchison and Dr. Penny Hamilton for your help. Thank you to everyone mentioned in Chasing Planes who was part of the adventures and to those who have supported me and my mission to save aviation history.